FOR ORGANS, PIANOS & ELECTRONIC KEYBOARDS

E-Z PLAY TODAY

104

Halle
& 40 More Great Songs

ISBN 978-1-4950-2611-9

HAL•LEONARD®
CORPORATION

7777 W. BLUEMOUND RD. P.O. BOX 13819 MILWAUKEE, WI 53213

E-Z Play ® TODAY Music Notation © 1975 HAL LEONARD CORPORATION
E-Z PLAY and EASY ELECTRONIC KEYBOARD MUSIC are registered trademarks of HAL LEONARD CORPORATION.

Visit Hal Leonard Online at
www.halleonard.com

Ain't No Sunshine

Registration 8
Rhythm: 8-Beat or Blues

Words and Music by
Bill Withers

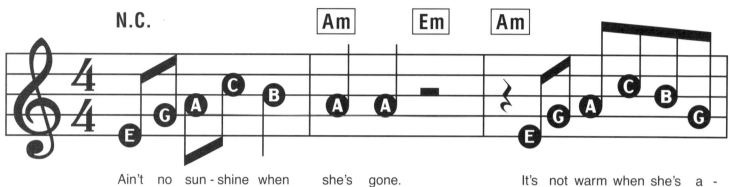

Ain't no sun-shine when she's gone. It's not warm when she's a-

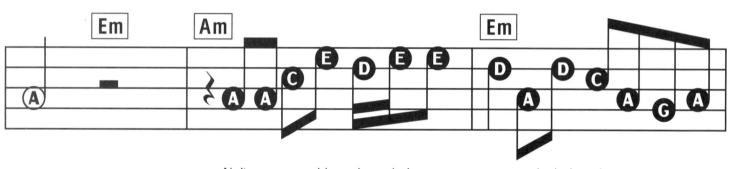

way. Ain't no sun-shine when she's gone, _____ and she's al-ways gone too

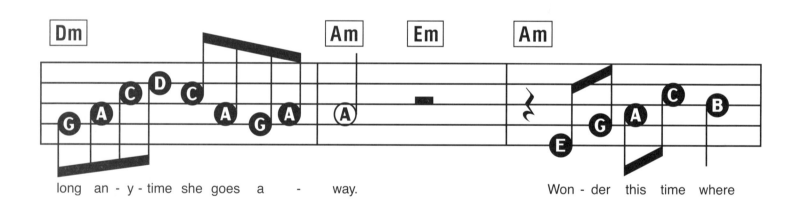

long an-y-time she goes a - way. Won-der this time where

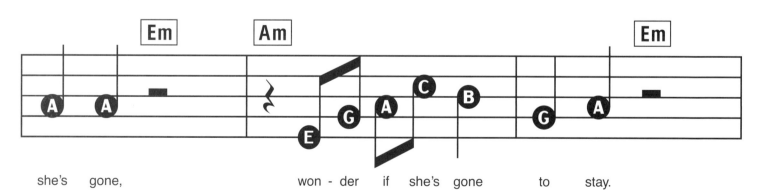

she's gone, won-der if she's gone to stay.

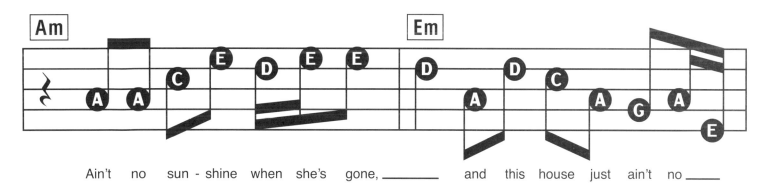

Ain't no sun - shine when she's gone, _____ and this house just ain't no _____

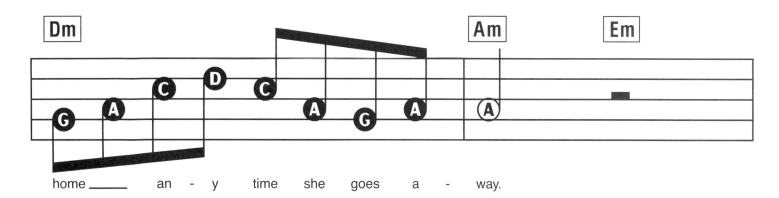

home _____ an - y time she goes a - way.

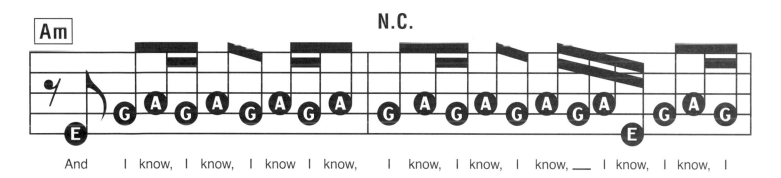

And I know, I know, I know I know, I know, I know, I know, ___ I know, I know, I

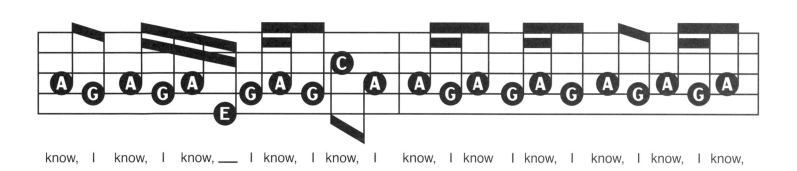

know, I know, I know, ___ I know, I know, I know, I know I know, I know, I know, I know,

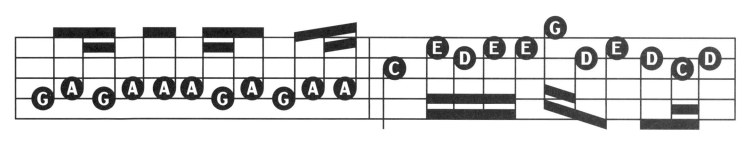

I know, I know, I know I know, I know, I know, hey, I ought to leave the young thing a - lone, _

6

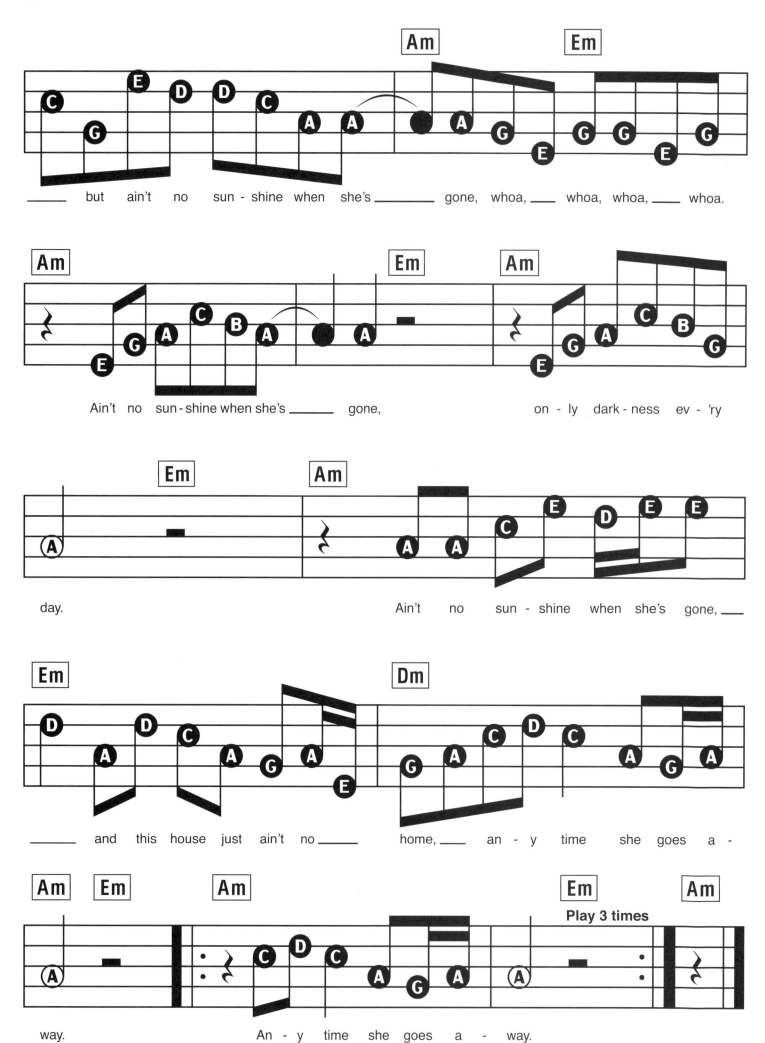

Cecilia

Registration 9
Rhythm: March or Rock

Words and Music by
Paul Simon

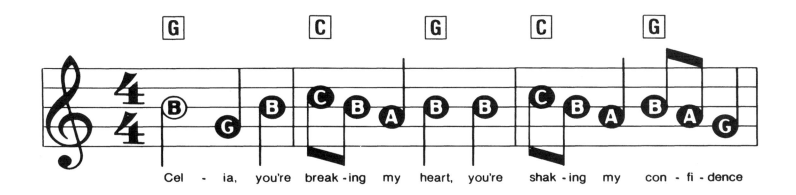

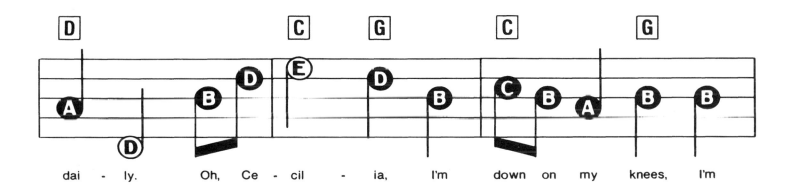

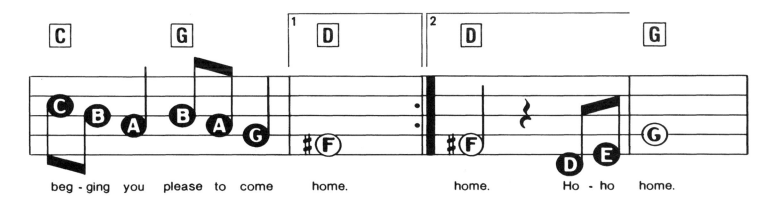

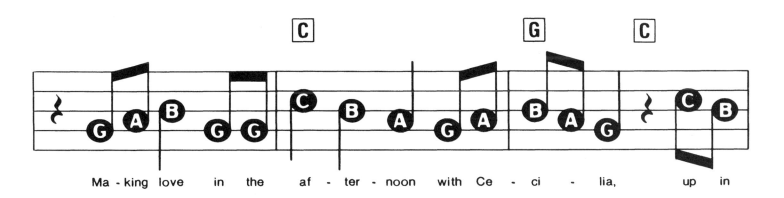

8

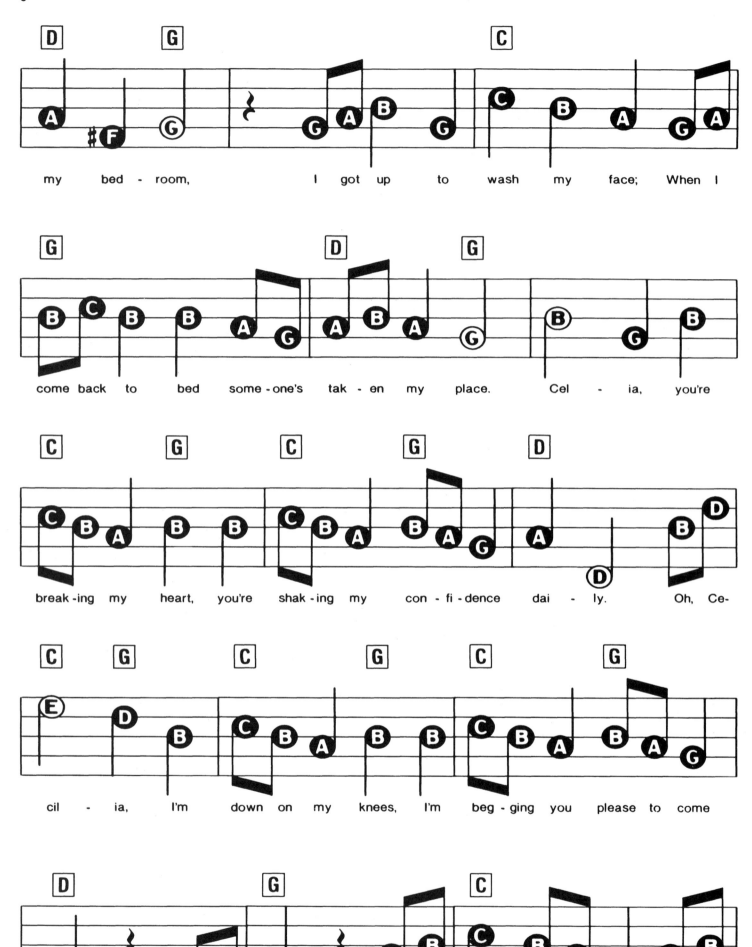

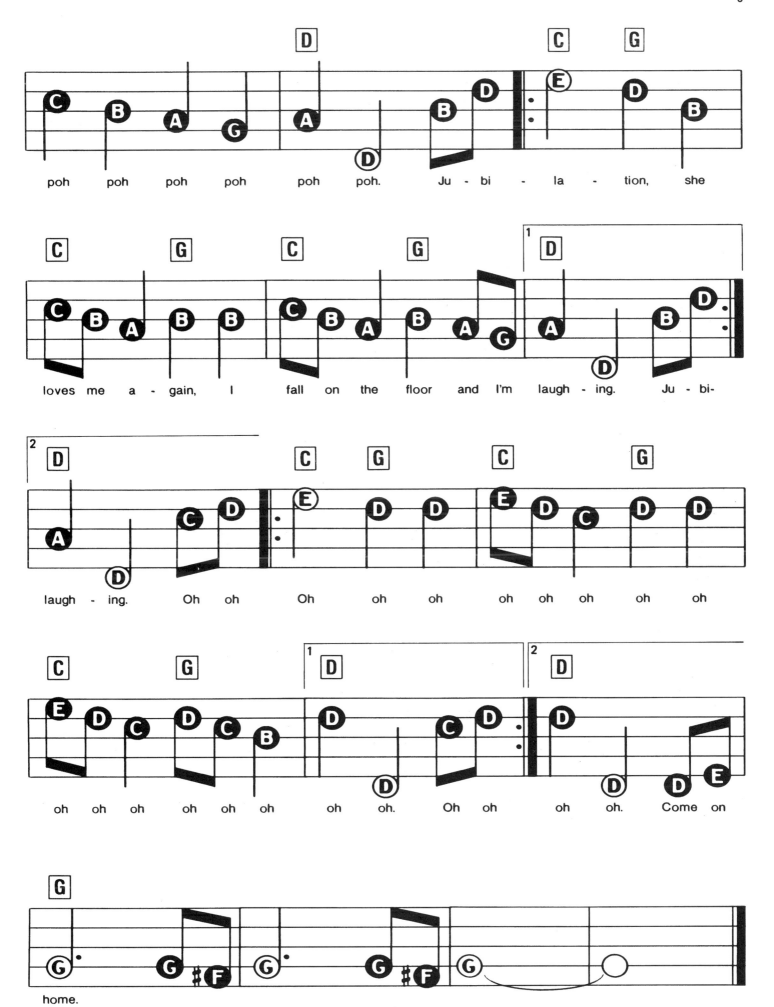

Alone Together

Registration 2
Rhythm: Ballad

Lyrics by Howard Dietz
Music by Arthur Schwartz

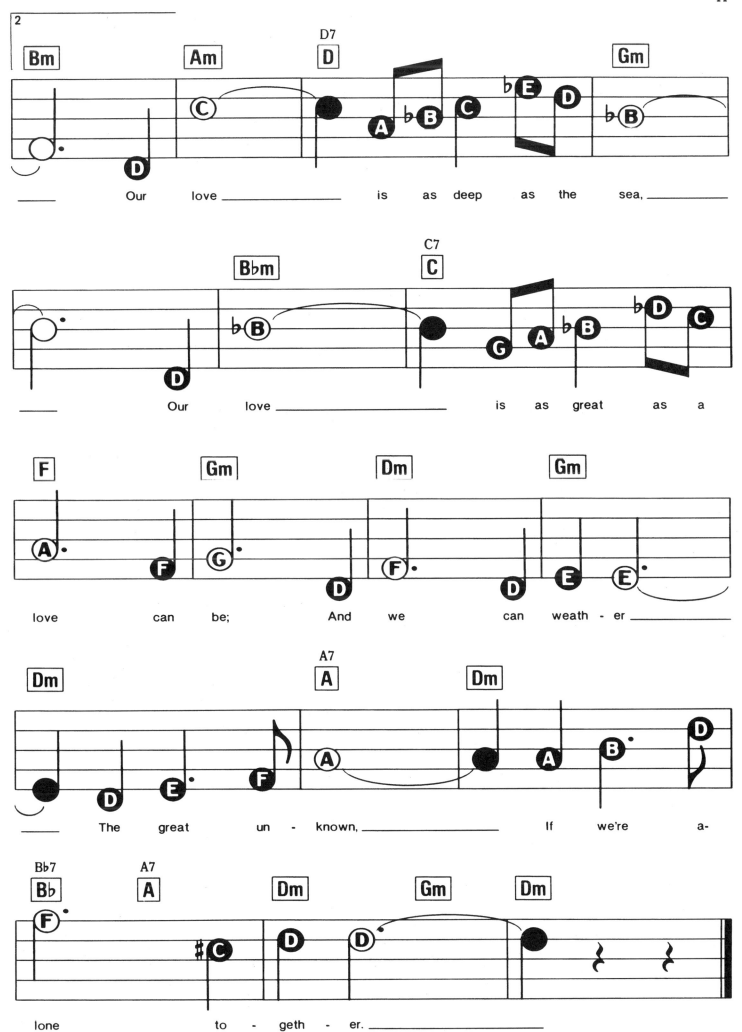

Blue Moon

Registration 8
Rhythm: Swing

Music by Richard Rodgers
Lyrics by Lorenz Hart

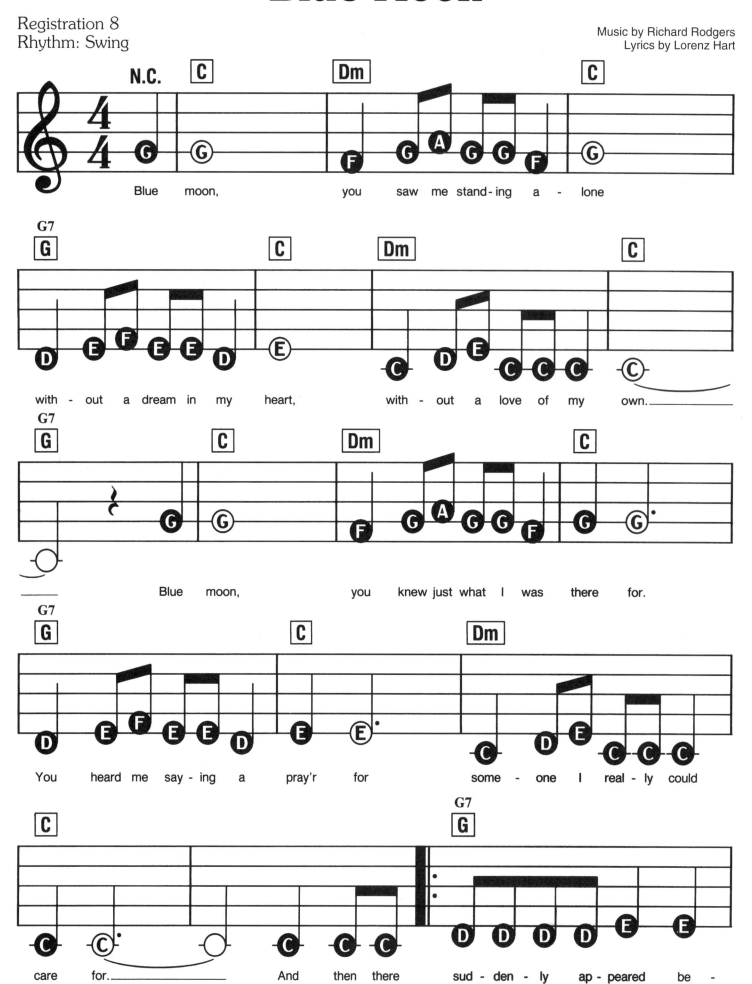

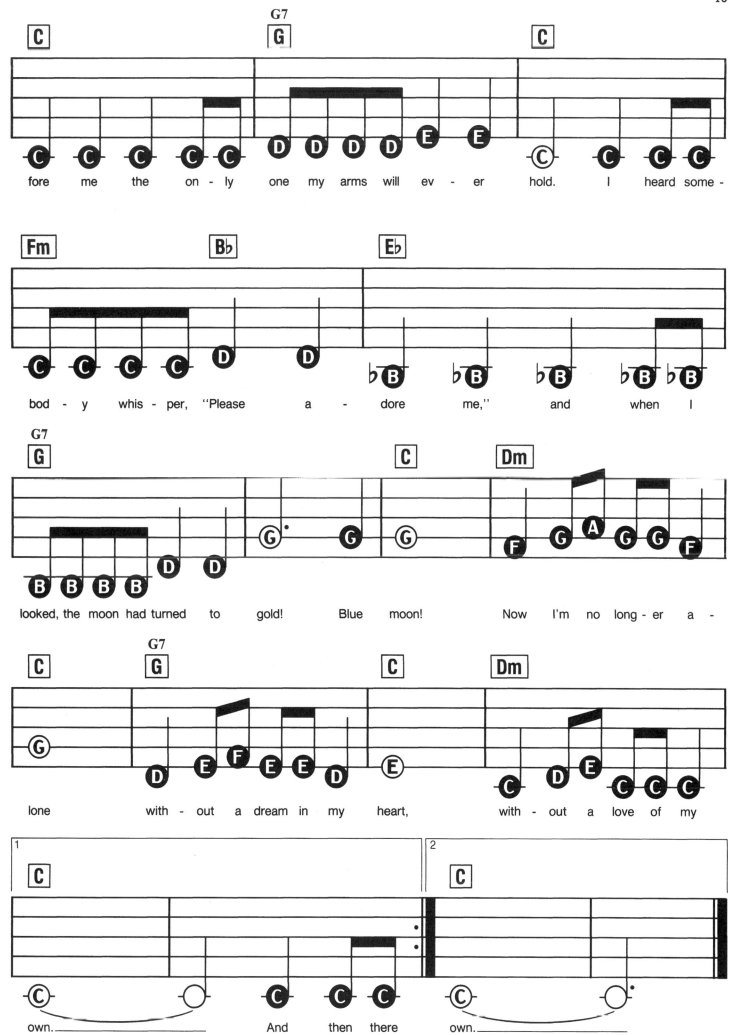

Chattanooga Choo Choo

Registration 9
Rhythm: Swing

Words by Mack Gordon
Music by Harry Warren

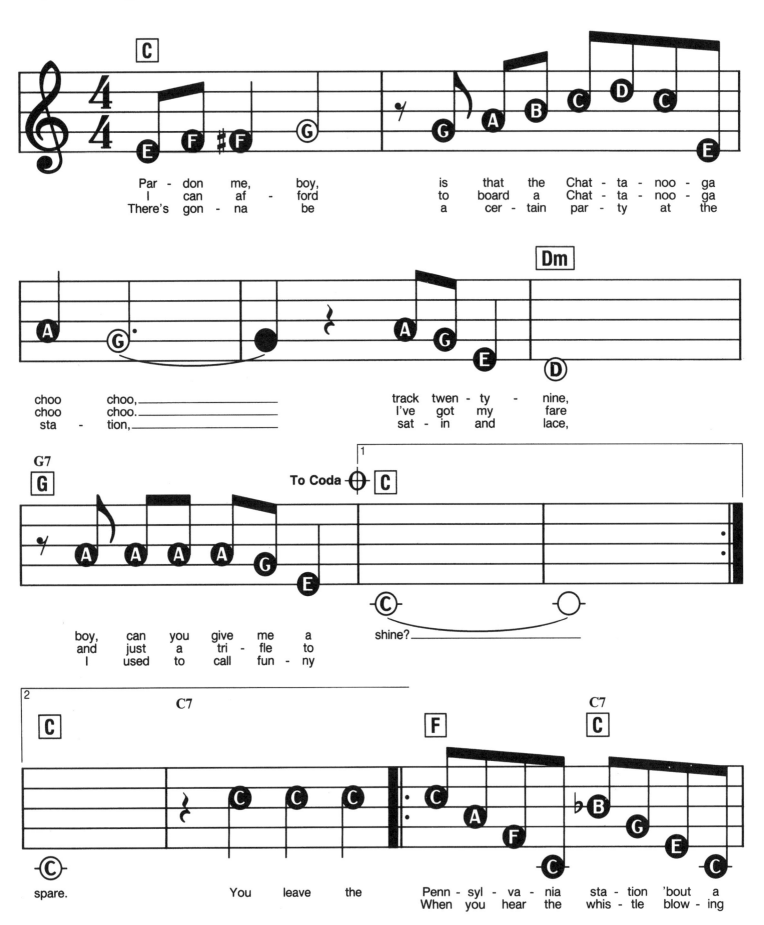

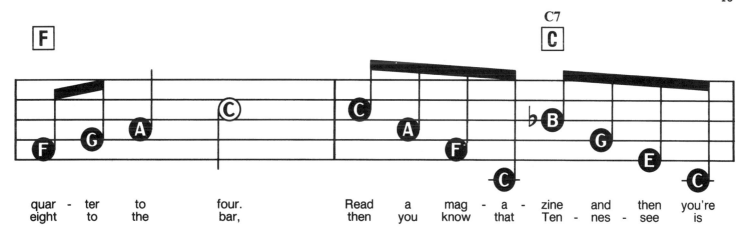

quar - ter to four.
eight to the bar,

Read a mag - a - zine and then you're
then you know that Ten - nes - see is

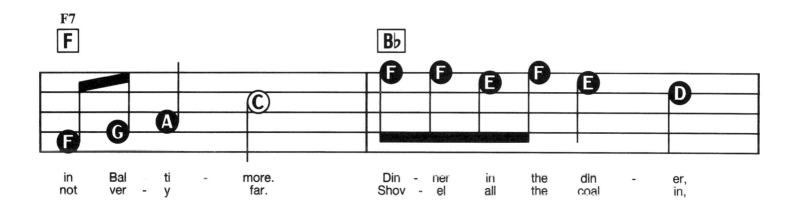

in Bal - ti - more.
not ver - y far.

Din - ner in the din - er,
Shov - el all the coal in,

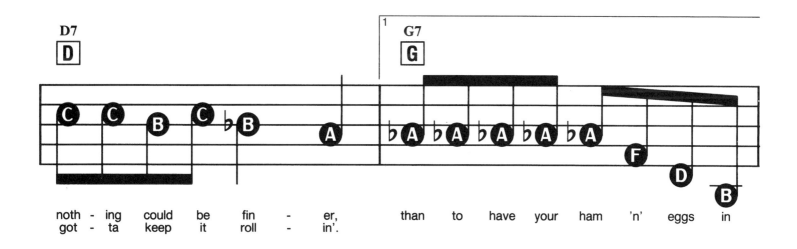

noth - ing could be fin - er,
got - ta keep it roll - in'.

than to have your ham 'n' eggs in

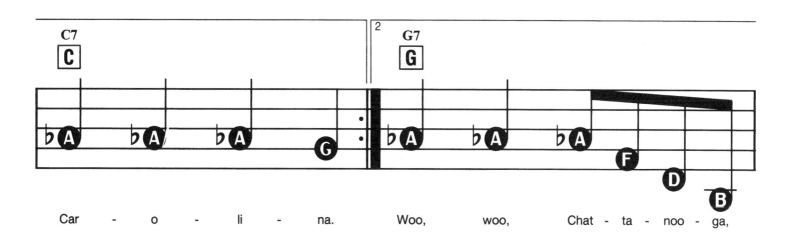

Car - o - li - na.

Woo, woo, Chat - ta - noo - ga,

16

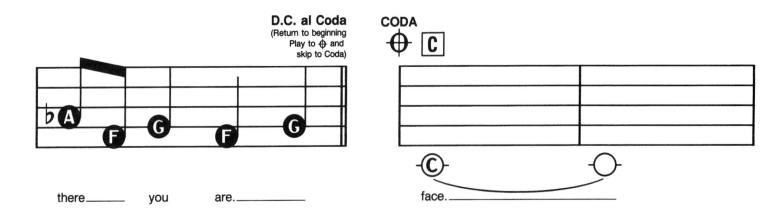

there_____ you are._____

face._____

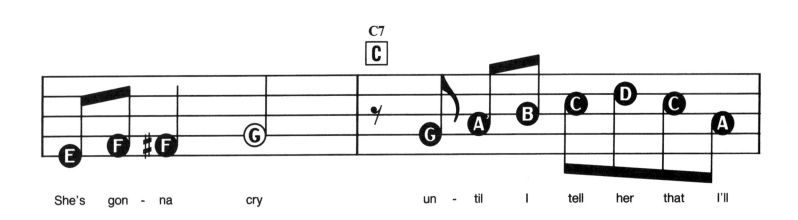

She's gon - na cry un - til I tell her that I'll

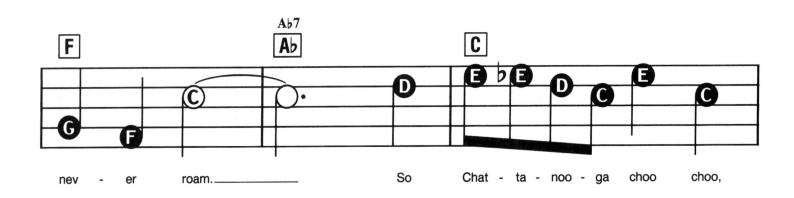

nev - er roam._____ So Chat - ta - noo - ga choo choo,

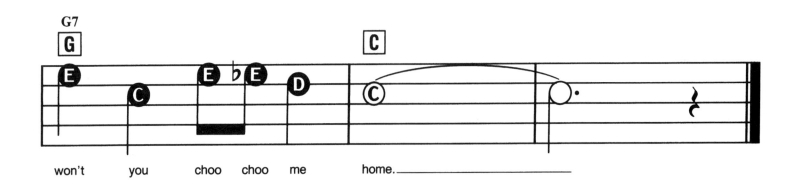

won't you choo choo me home._____

Do You Believe in Magic

Registration 4
Rhythm: Country

Words and Music by
John Sebastian

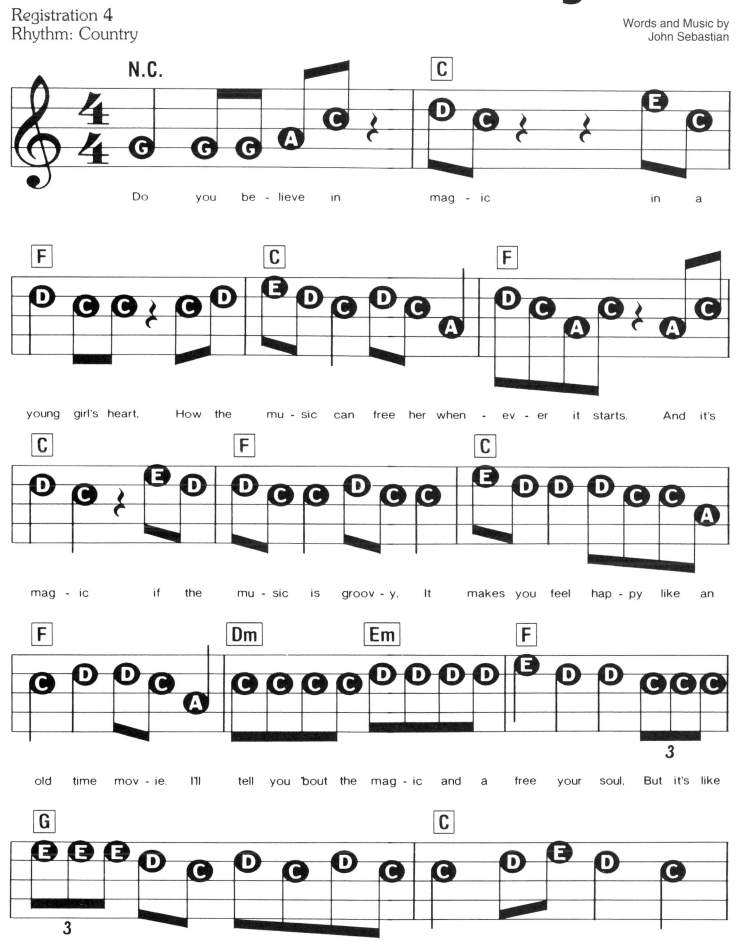

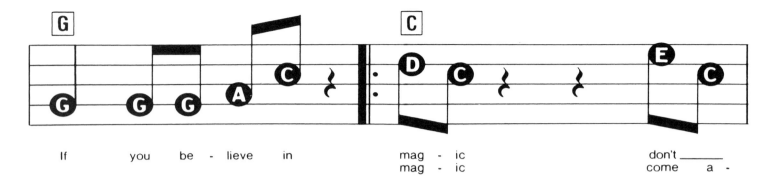

If you be - lieve in mag - ic don't _____
mag - ic come a -

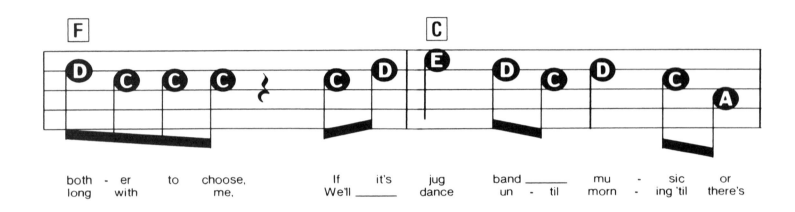

both - er to choose, If it's jug band _____ mu - sic or
long with me, We'll _____ dance un - til morn - ing 'til there's

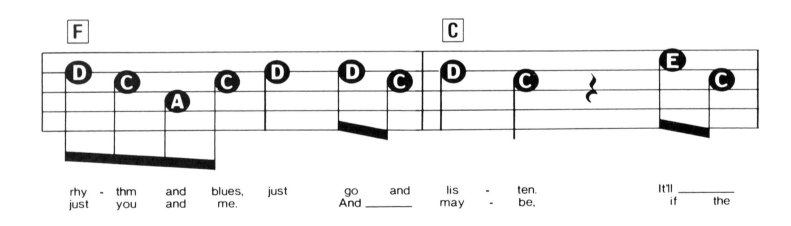

rhy - thm and blues, just go and lis - ten. It'll _____
just you and me. And _____ may - be, if the

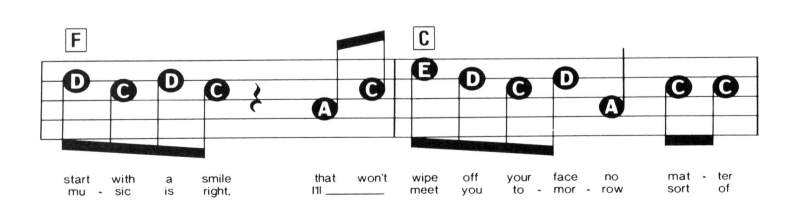

start with a smile that won't wipe off your face no mat - ter
mu - sic is right, I'll _____ meet you to - mor - row sort of

19

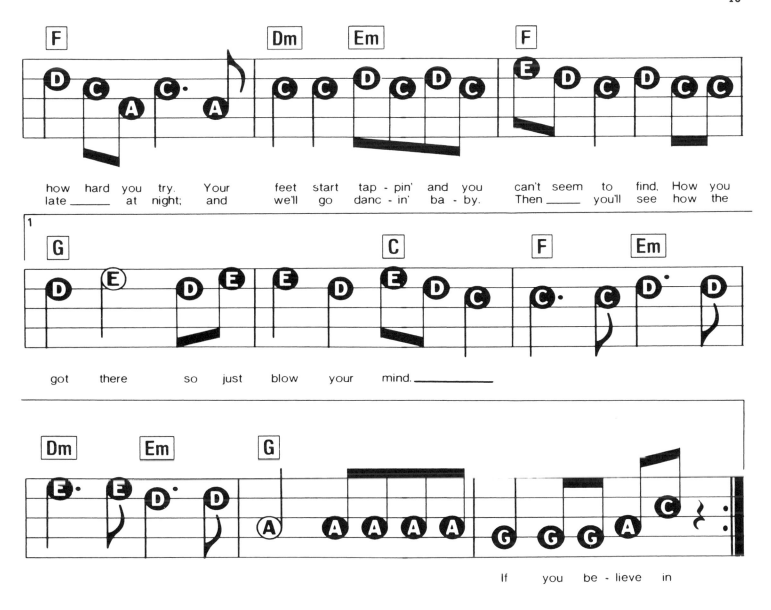

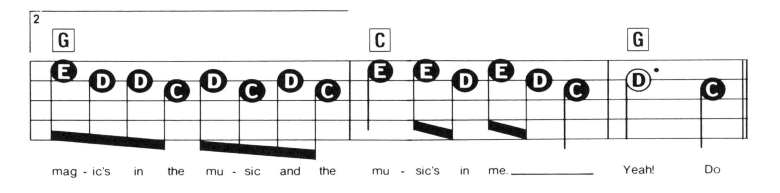

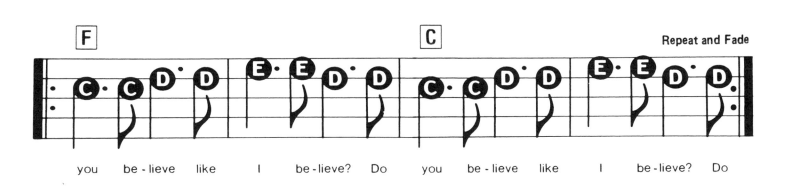

Emily
from the MGM Motion Picture THE AMERICANIZATION OF EMILY

Registration 3
Rhythm: Waltz

Music by Johnny Mandel
Words by Johnny Mercer

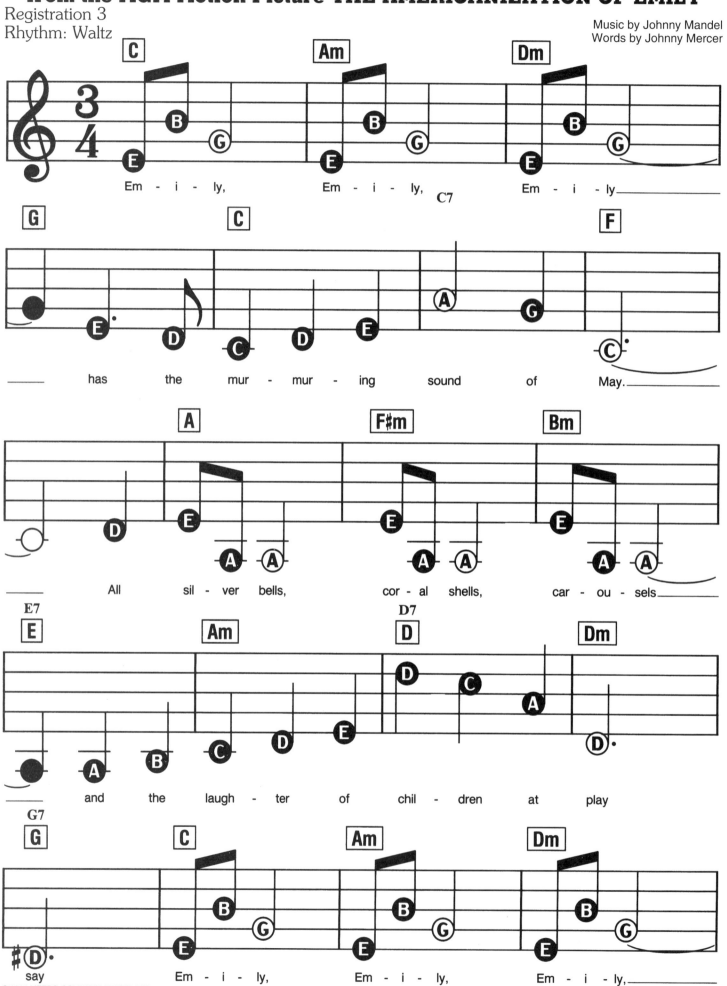

Hallelujah

Registration 4
Rhythm: 6/8 March

Words and Music by
Leonard Cohen

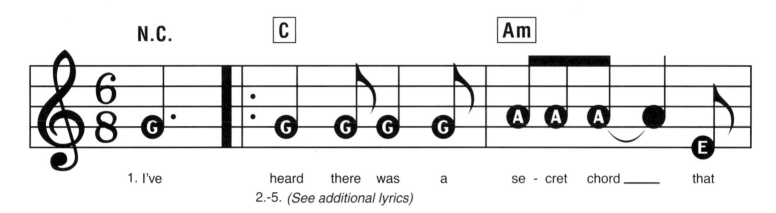

1. I've heard there was a se-cret chord ____ that
2.-5. *(See additional lyrics)*

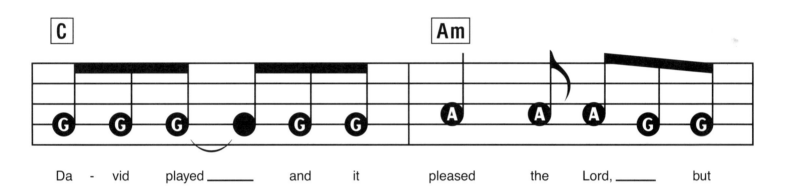

Da - vid played ____ and it pleased the Lord, ____ but

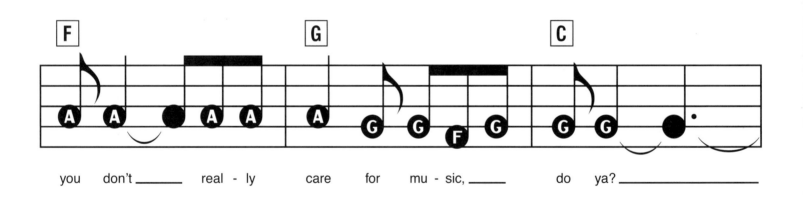

you don't ____ real - ly care for mu - sic, ____ do ya? ____

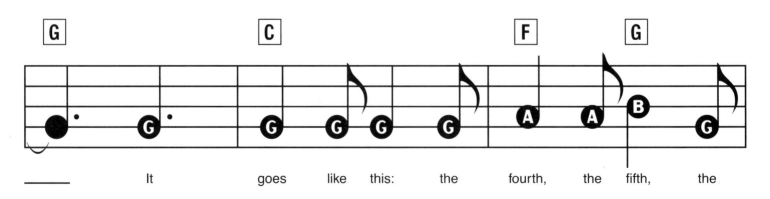

____ It goes like this: the fourth, the fifth, the

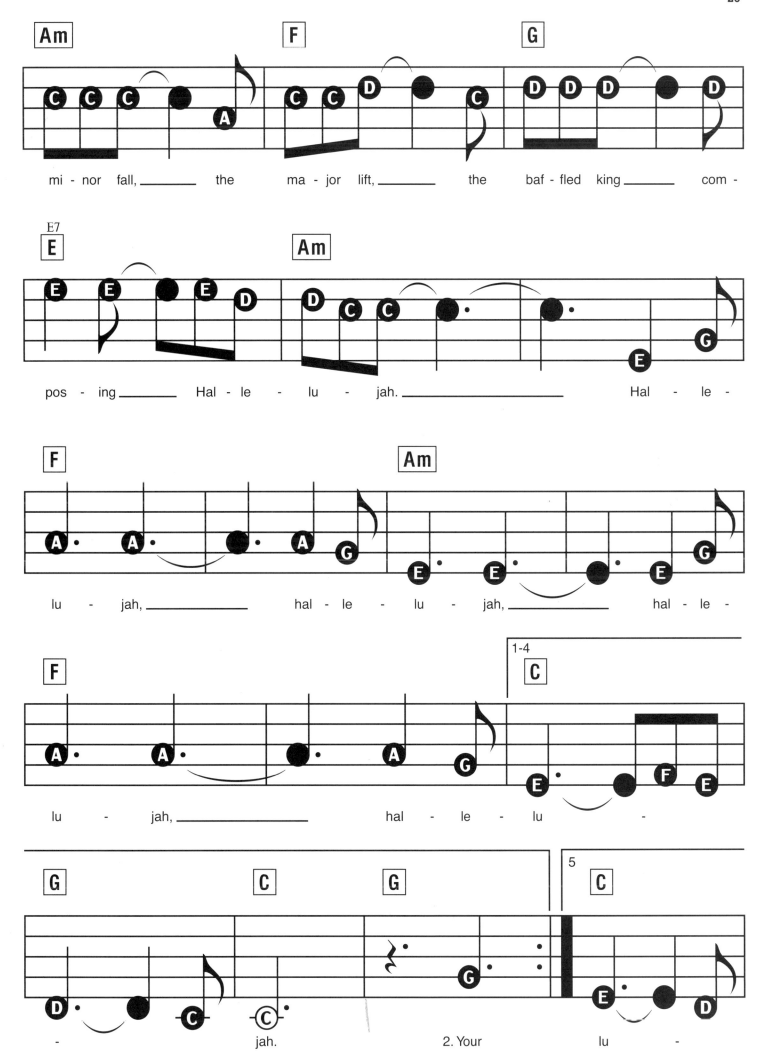

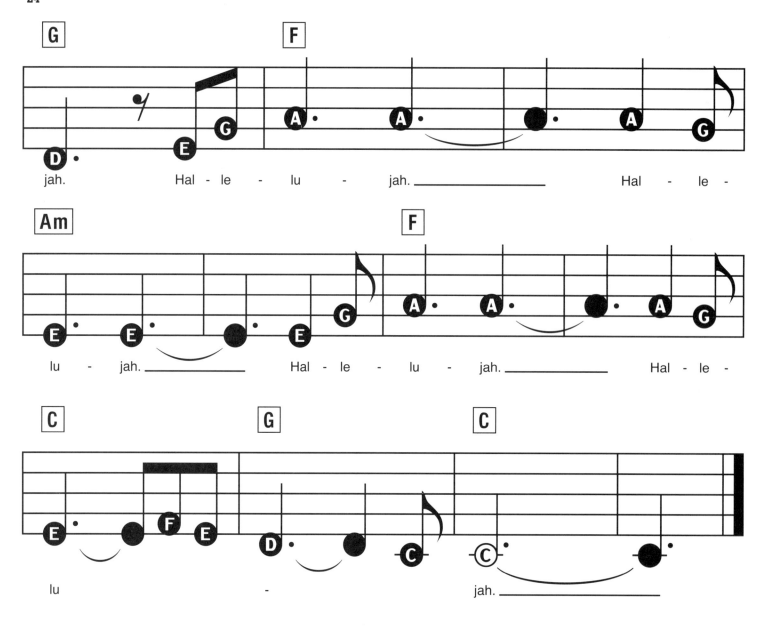

Additional Lyrics

2. Your faith was strong but you needed proof.
   You saw her bathing on the roof.
   Her beauty and the moonlight overthrew ya.
   She tied you to a kitchen chair.
   She broke your throne, she cut your hair.
   And from your lips she drew the Hallelujah.

3. Maybe I have been here before.
   I know this room, I've walked this floor.
   I used to live alone before I knew ya.
   I've seen your flag on the marble arch.
   Love is not a vict'ry march.
   It's a cold and it's a broken Hallelujah.

4. There was a time you let me know
   What's real and going on below.
   But now you never show it to me, do ya?
   And remember when I moved in you.
   The holy dark was movin', too,
   And every breath we drew was Hallelujah.

5. Maybe there's a God above,
   And all I ever learned from love
   Was how to shoot at someone who outdrew ya.
   And it's not a cry you can hear at night.
   It's not somebody who's seen the light.
   It's a cold and it's a broken Hallelujah.

Happy Days Are Here Again

Registration 2
Rhythm: Fox Trot or Swing

Words and Music by Jack Yellen
and Milton Ager

Hap - py days _____ are here a - gain! _____

_____ The skies a - bove _____ are clear a - gain. _____

_____ Let us sing a song _____ of cheer a - gain, _____

_____ hap - py days are here a - gain!

All to - geth - er, shout it now! _____

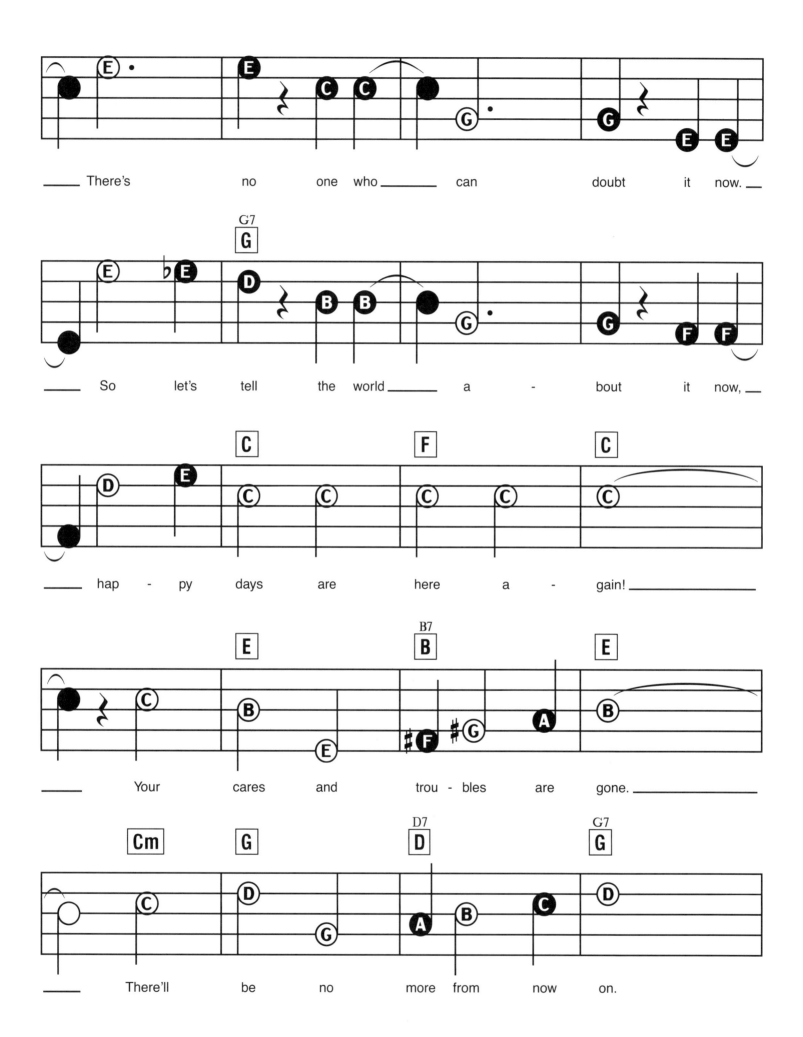

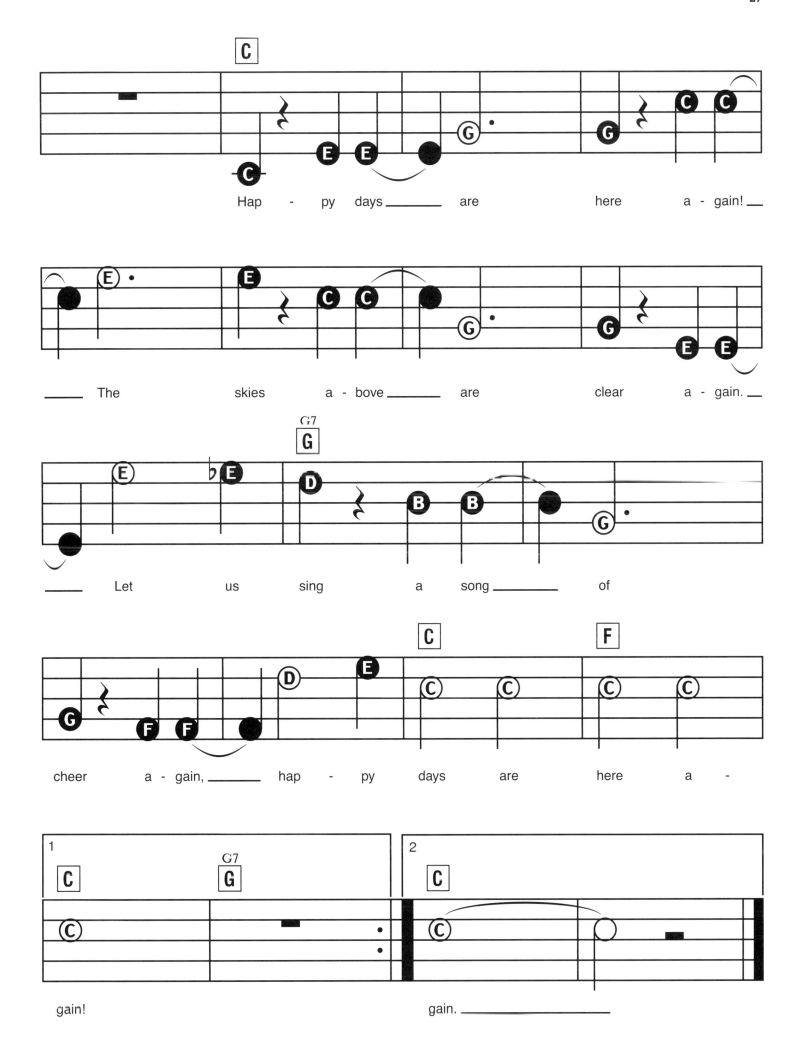

Hey There
from THE PAJAMA GAME

Registration 2
Rhythm: Fox Trot

Words and Music by Richard Adler
and Jerry Ross

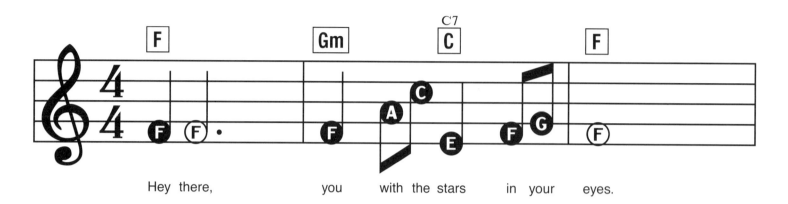

Hey there, you with the stars in your eyes.

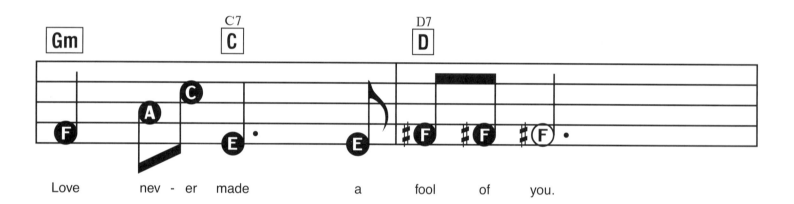

Love nev - er made a fool of you.

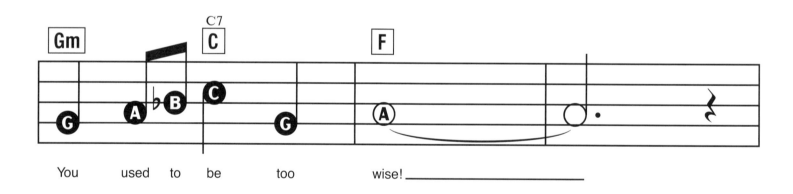

You used to be too wise! _____

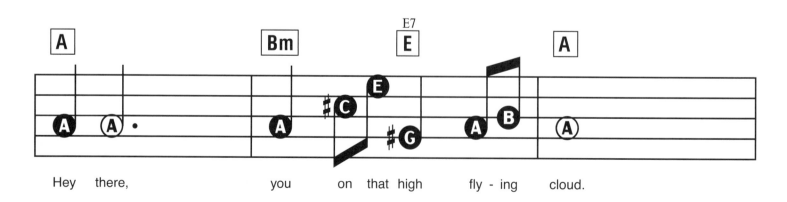

Hey there, you on that high fly - ing cloud.

29

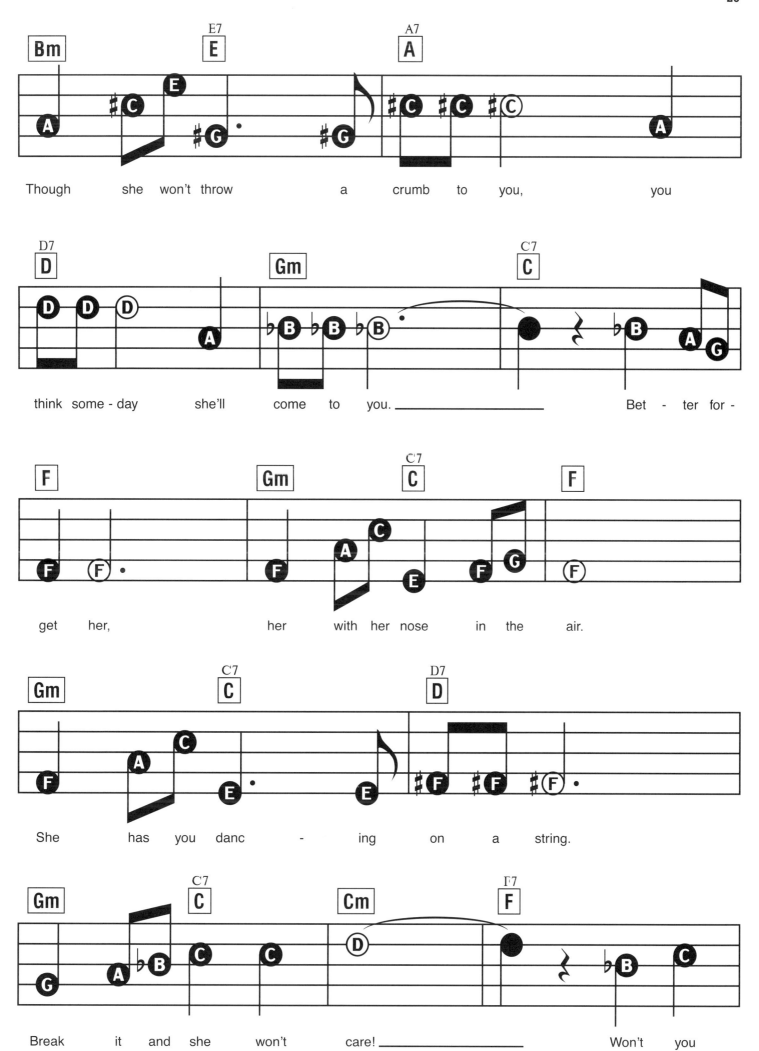

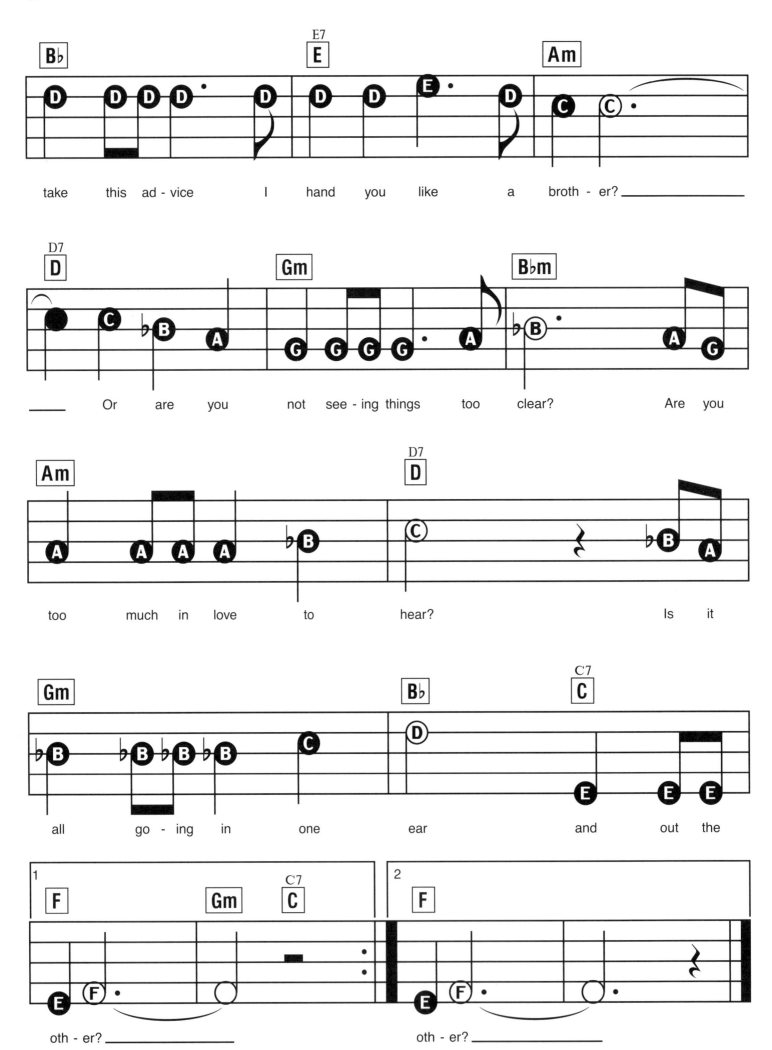

I Got You Babe

Registration 5
Rhythm: Slow Rock or 12-Beat

Words and Music by
Sonny Bono

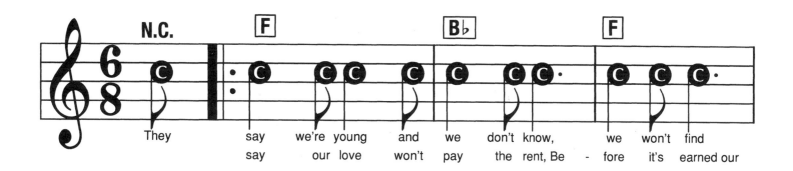

They
say

say
we're young and we don't know,
our love won't pay the rent, Be -
we won't find
fore it's earned our

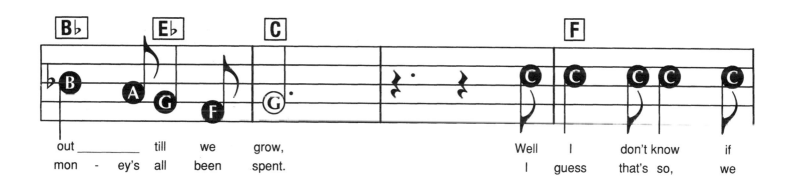

out _____ till we grow,
mon - ey's all been spent.
Well I don't know if
I guess that's so, we

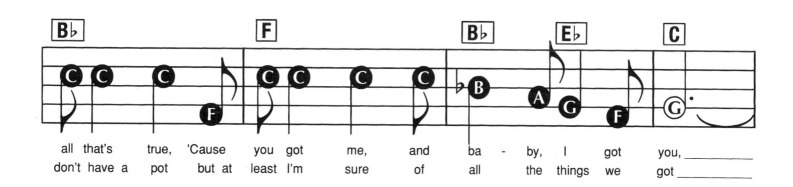

all that's true, 'Cause you got me, and ba - by, I got you, _____
don't have a pot but at least I'm sure of all the things we got _____

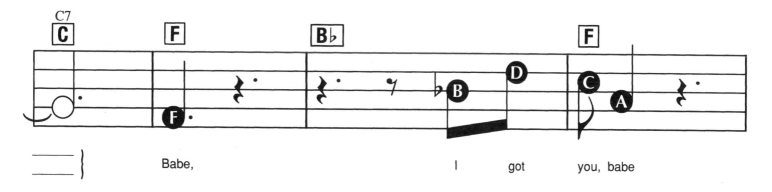

_____ }
Babe,
I got you, babe

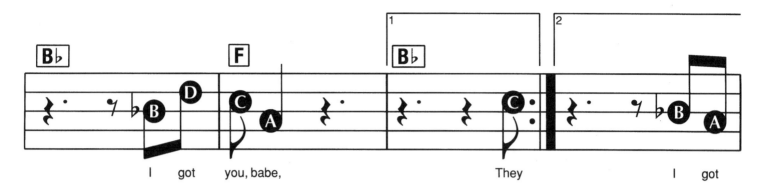

I got you, babe,   They   I got

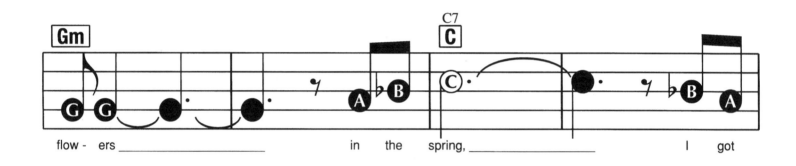

flow - ers _____ in the spring, _____ I got

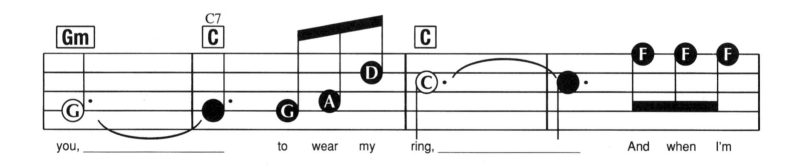

you, _____ to wear my ring, _____ And when I'm

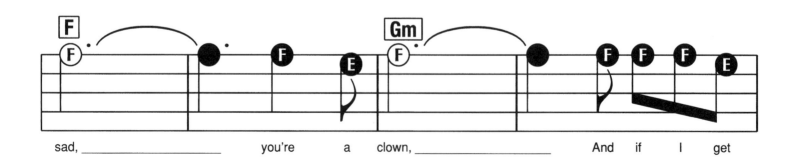

sad, _____ you're a clown, _____ And if I get

33

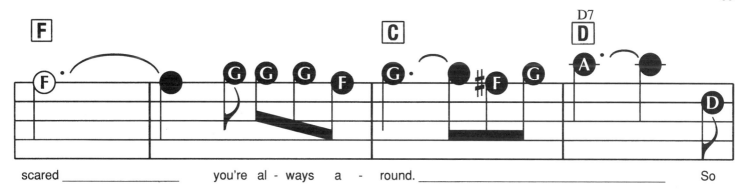

scared _____ you're al - ways a - round. _____ So

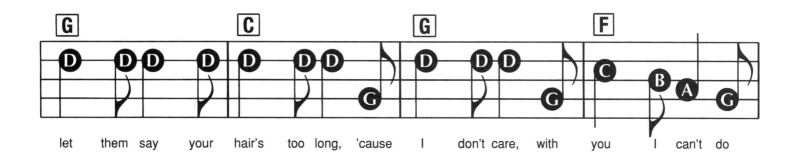

let them say your hair's too long, 'cause I don't care, with you I can't do

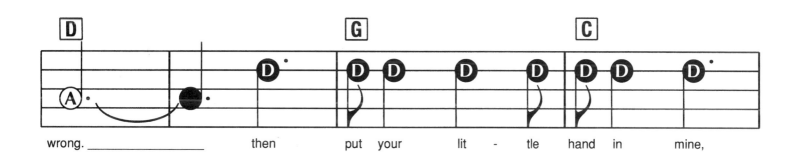

wrong. _____ then put your lit - tle hand in mine,

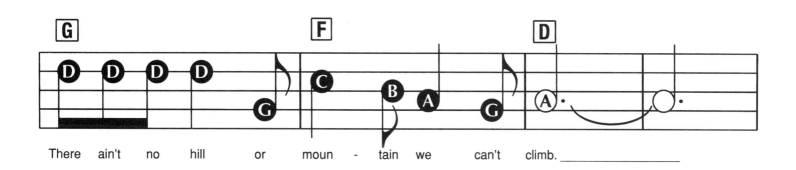

There ain't no hill or moun - tain we can't climb. _____

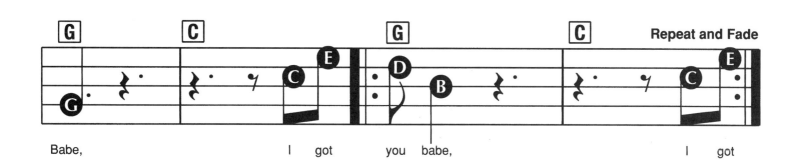

Babe, I got you babe, I got

The House of the Rising Sun

Registration 4
Rhythm: Waltz

Words and Music by
Alan Price

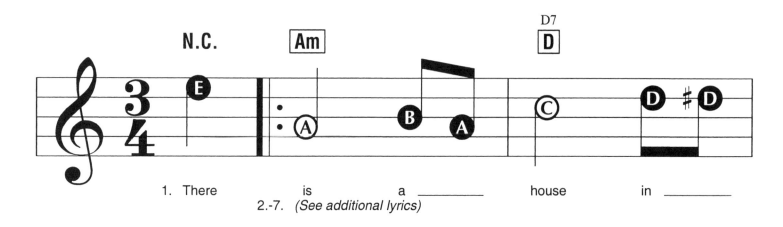

1. There is a _____ house in _____
2.-7. *(See additional lyrics)*

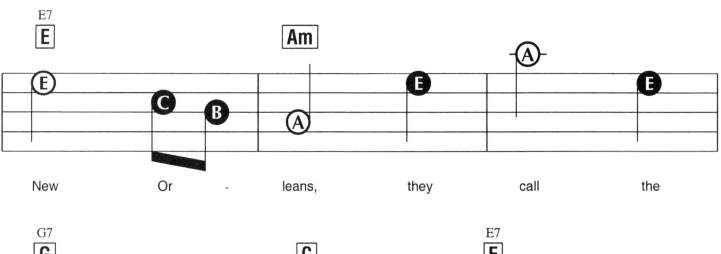

New Or - leans, they call the

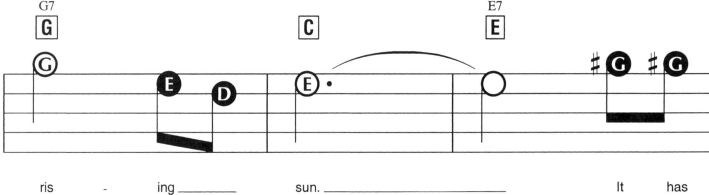

ris - ing _____ sun. _____ It has

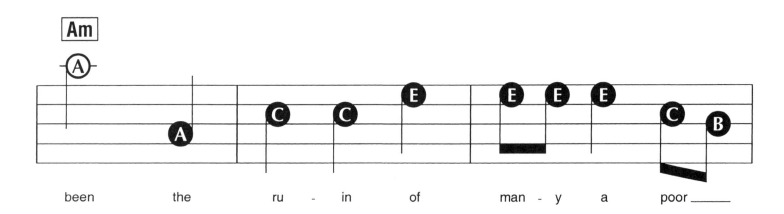

been the ru - in of man - y a poor ____

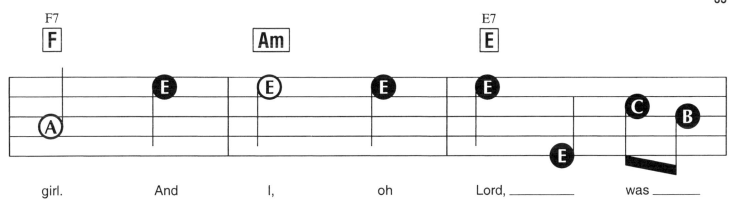

girl.   And   I,   oh   Lord, _____   was _____

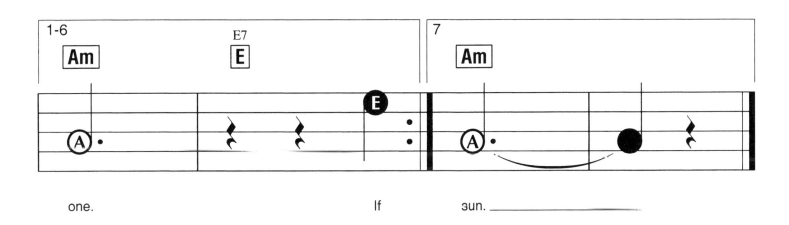

one.   If   sun. _____

Additional Lyrics

2. If I had listened to what mama said,
   I'd 'a' been at home today.
   Being so young and foolish, poor girl,
   Let a gambler lead me astray.

3. My mother, she's a tailor,
   She sells those new blue jeans.
   My sweetheart, he's a drunkard, Lord,
   Drinks down in New Orleans.

4. The only thing a drunkard needs
   Is a suitcase and a trunk.
   The only time he's satisfied
   Is when he's on a drunk.

5. Go tell my baby, sister,
   Never do like I have done.
   To shun that house in New Orleans,
   They call the Rising Sun.

6. One foot is on the platform,
   And the other one on the train.
   I'm going back to New Orleans
   To wear that ball and chain.

7. I'm going back to New Orleans,
   My race is almost run.
   Going back to end my life
   Beneath the rising sun.

How About You?

Registration 9
Rhythm: Swing

Words by Ralph Freed
Music by Burton Lane

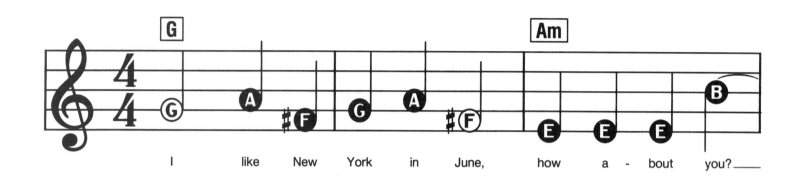

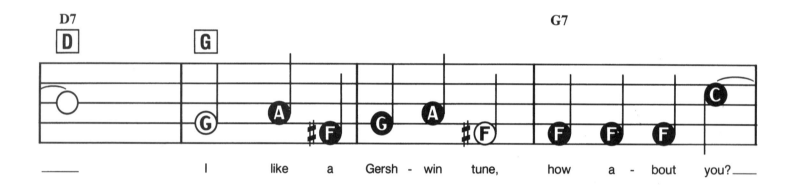

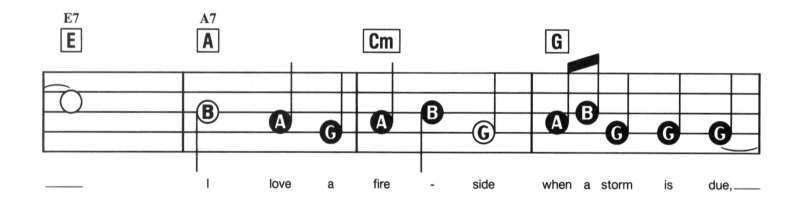

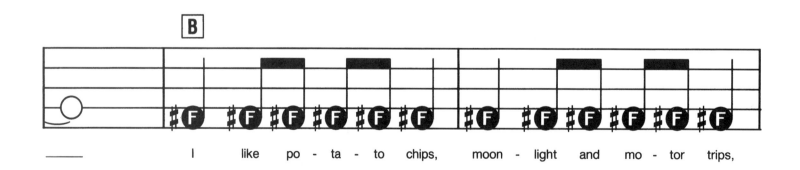

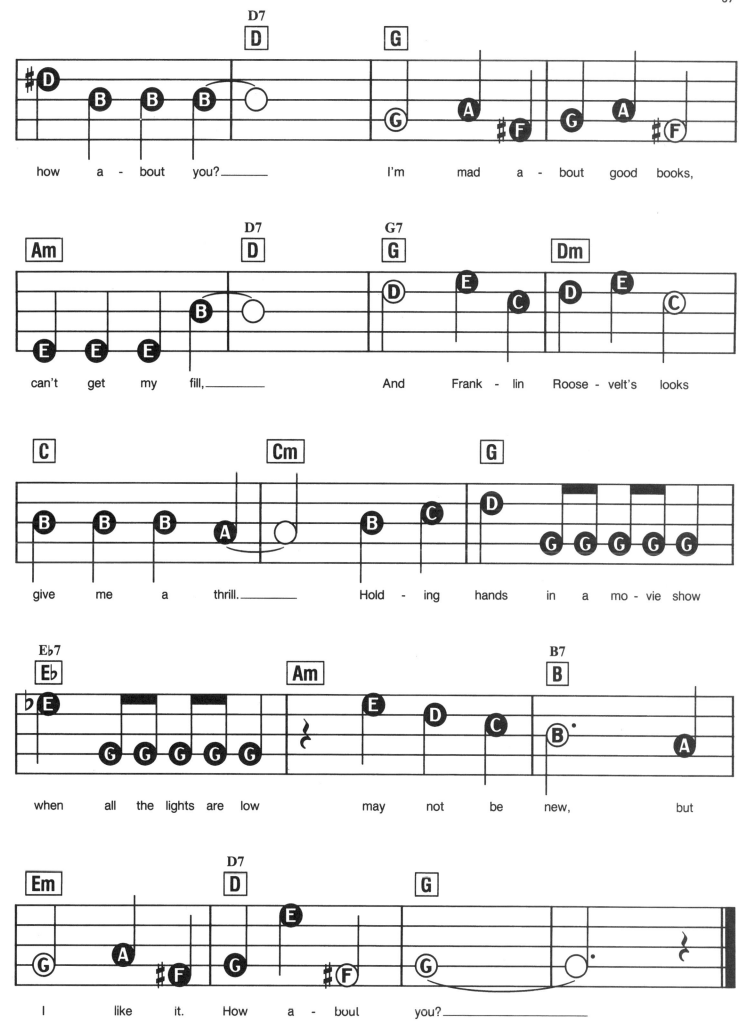

I Only Have Eyes for You

Registration 3
Rhythm: Fox Trot or Swing

Words by Al Dubin
Music by Harry Warren

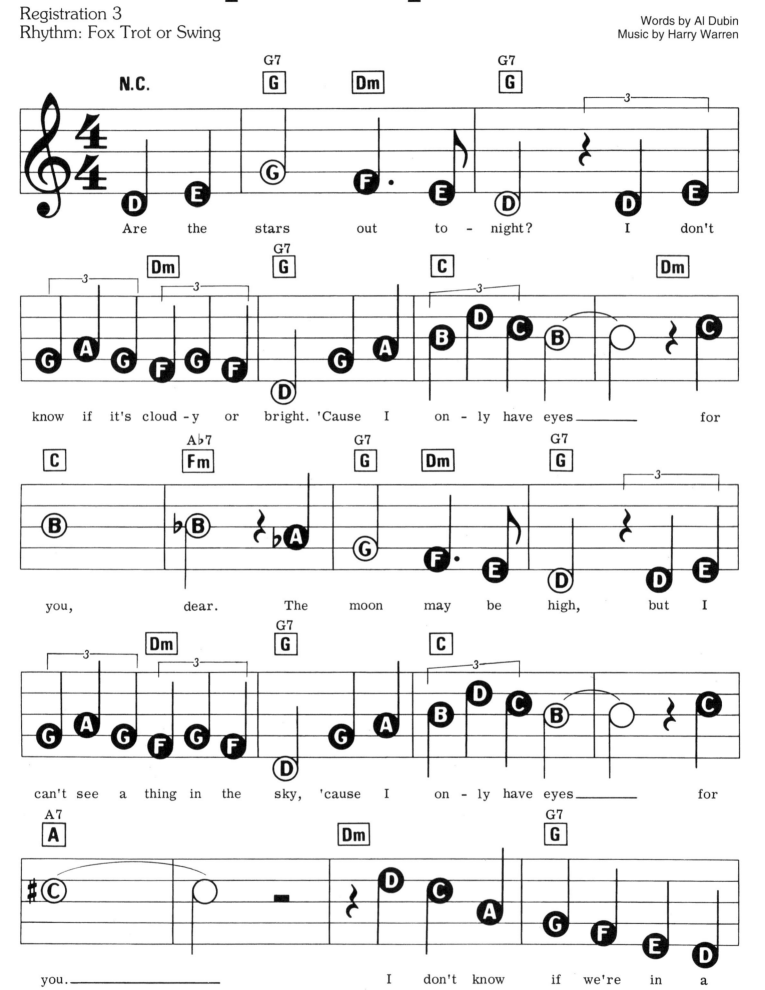

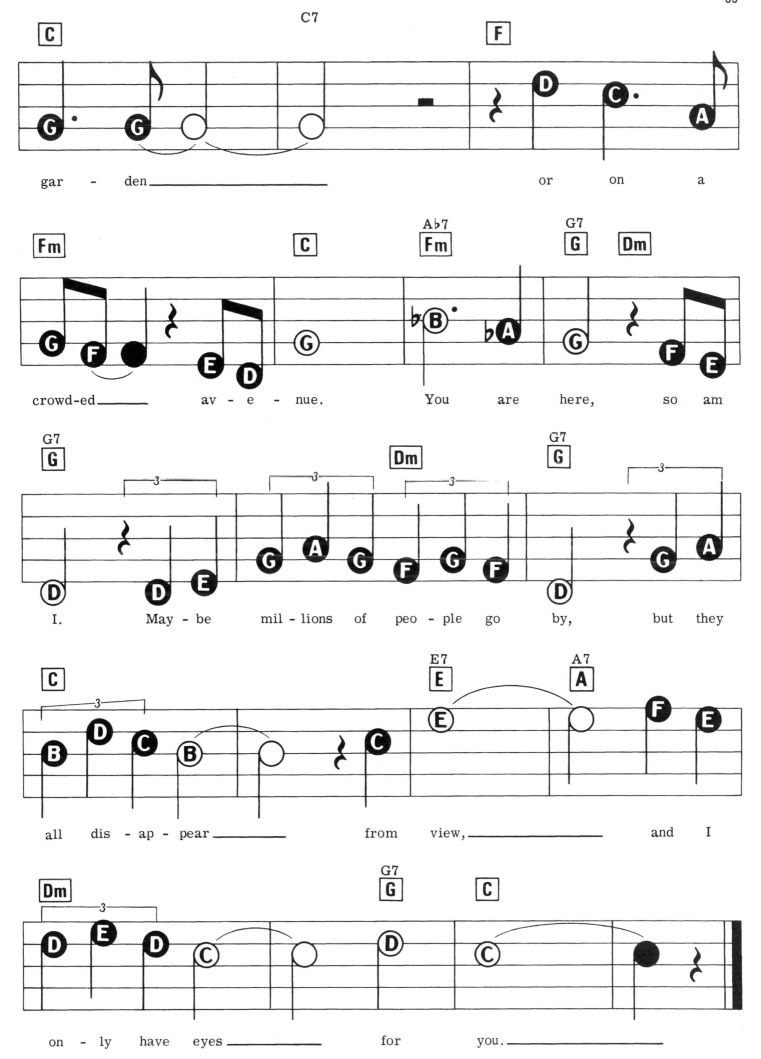

I'm in the Mood for Love

Registration 9
Rhythm: Fox Trot or Pops

Words and Music by Jimmy McHugh
and Dorothy Fields

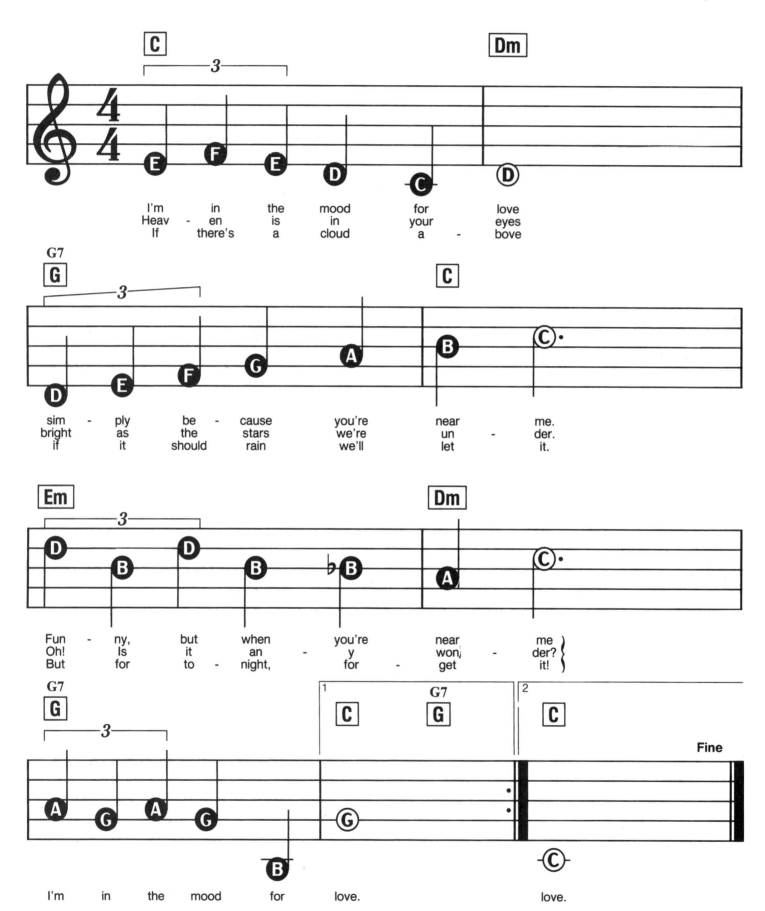

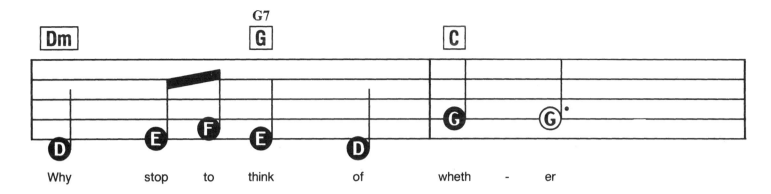

Why stop to think of wheth - er

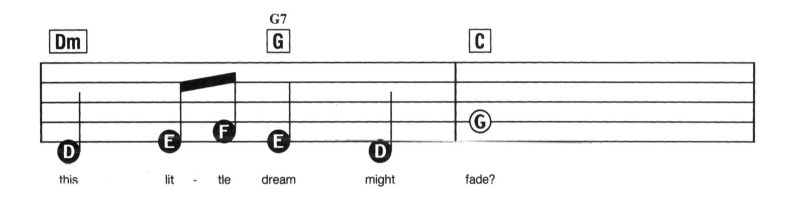

this lit - tle dream might fade?

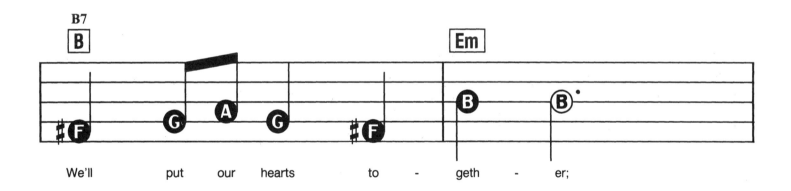

We'll put our hearts to - geth - er;

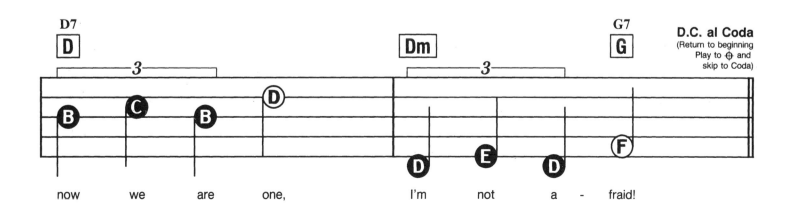

now we are one, I'm not a - fraid!

D.C. al Coda
(Return to beginning
Play to ⊕ and
skip to Coda)

Isn't She Lovely

Registration 8
Rhythm: Swing or Shuffle

Words and Music by
Stevie Wonder

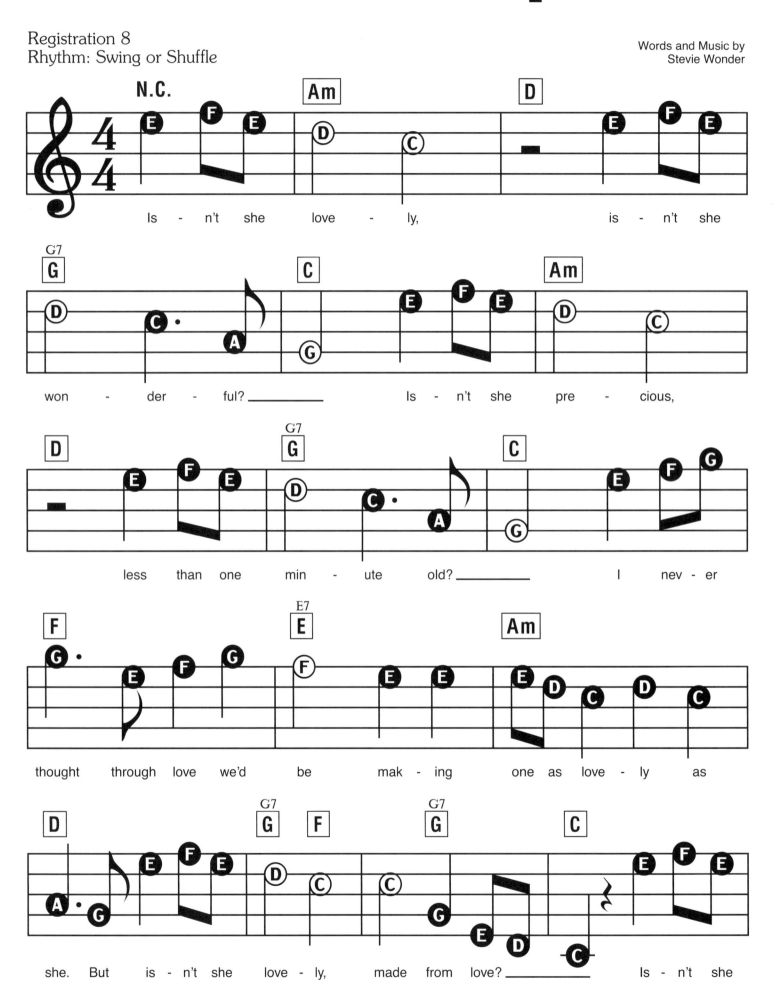

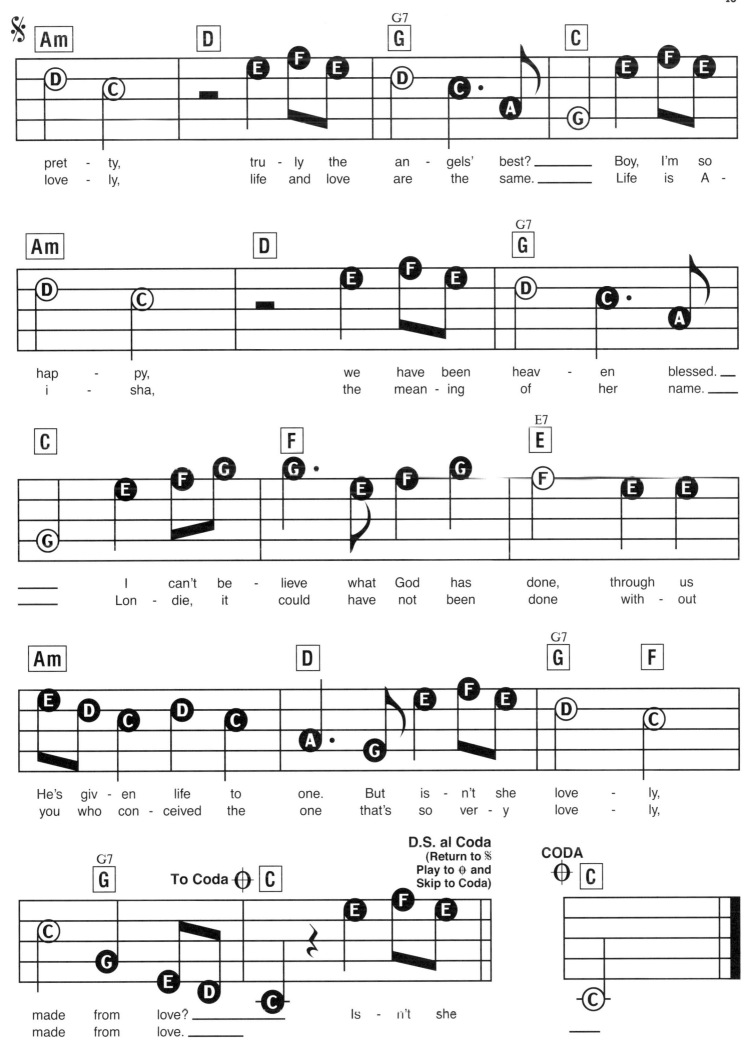

It Had to Be You

Registration 9
Rhythm: Swing

Words by Gus Kahn
Music by Isham Jones

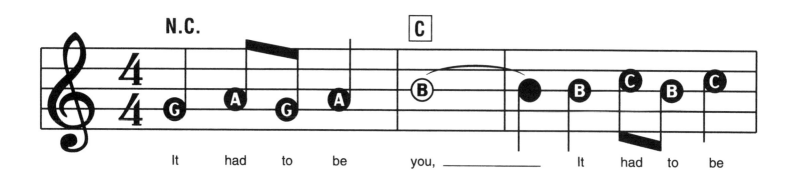

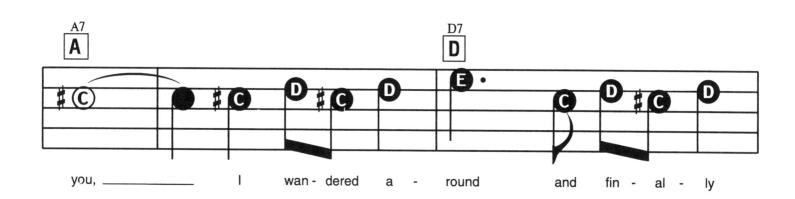

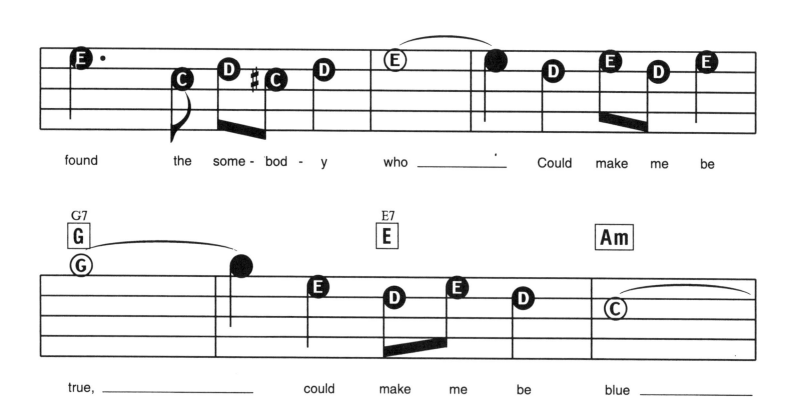

45

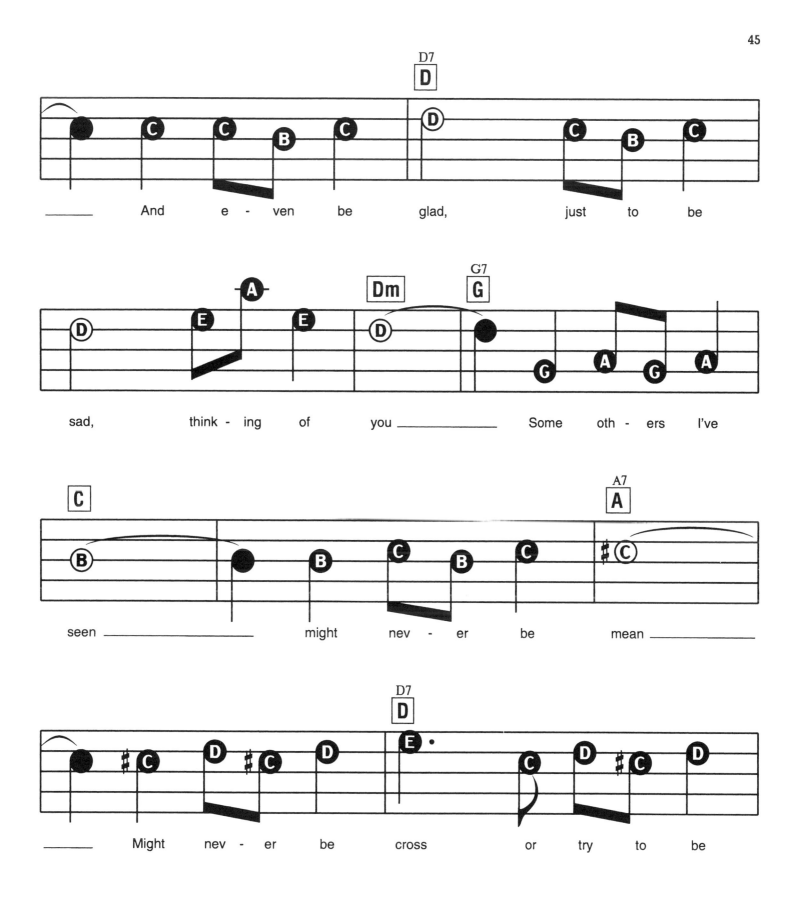

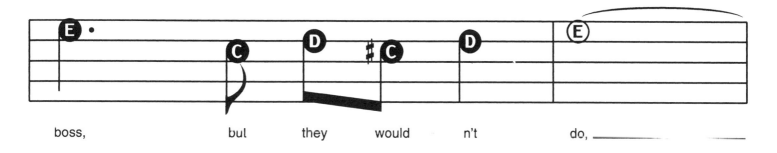

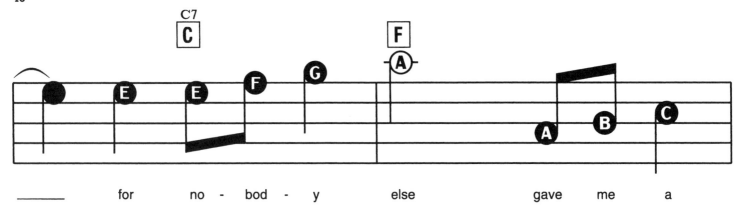

for no - bod - y else gave me a

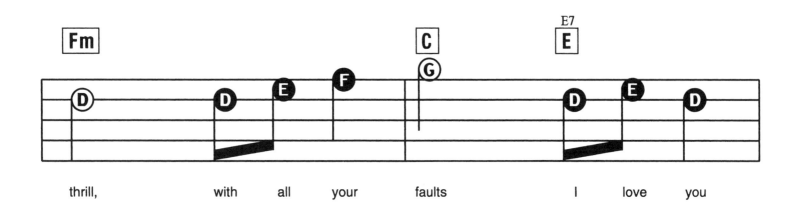

thrill, with all your faults I love you

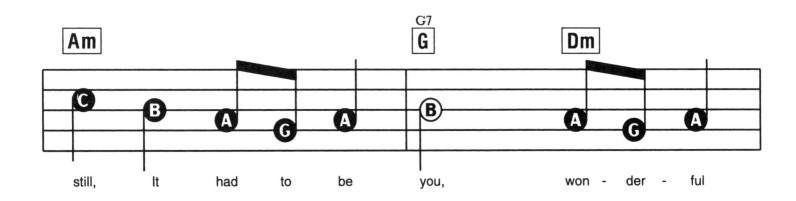

still, It had to be you, won - der - ful

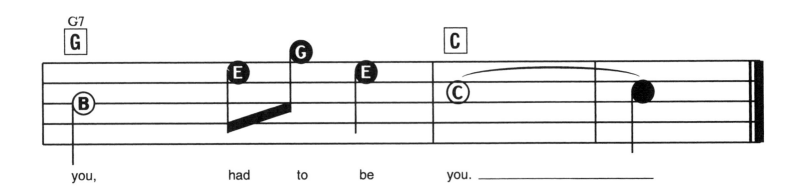

you, had to be you. _____

Man in the Mirror

Registration 5
Rhythm: Rock

Words and Music by Glen Ballard
and Siedah Garrett

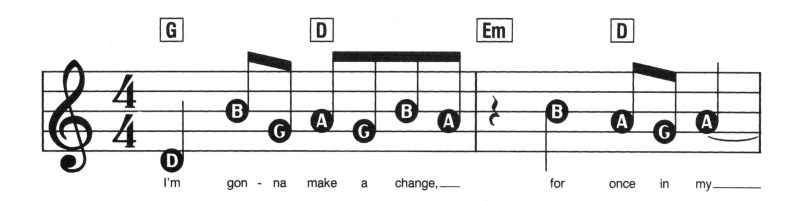

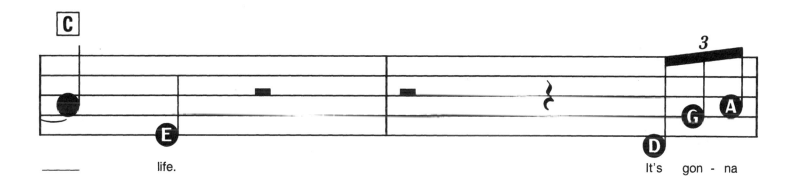

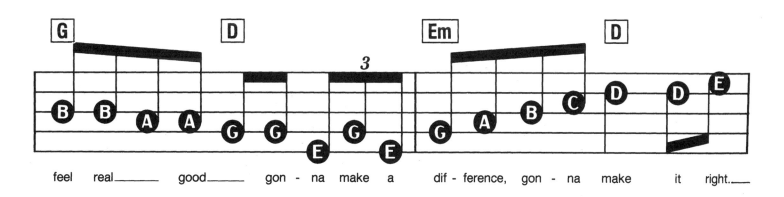

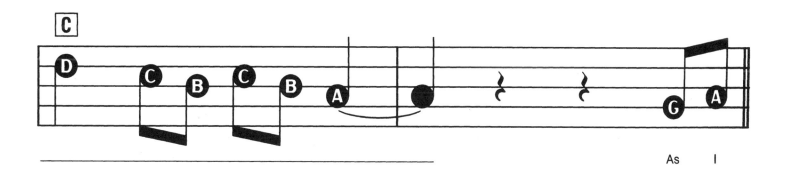

48

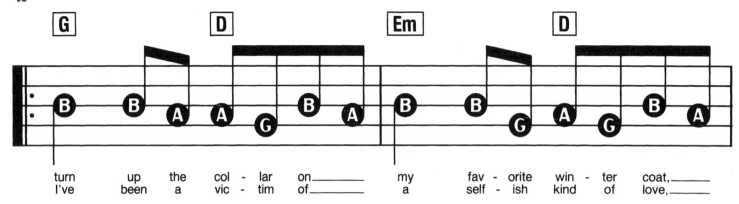

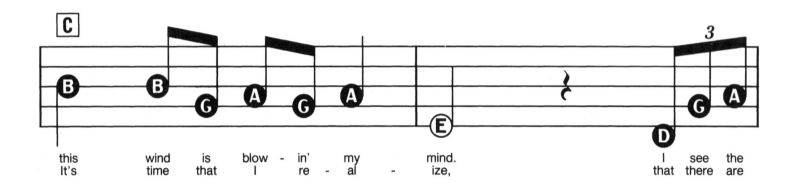

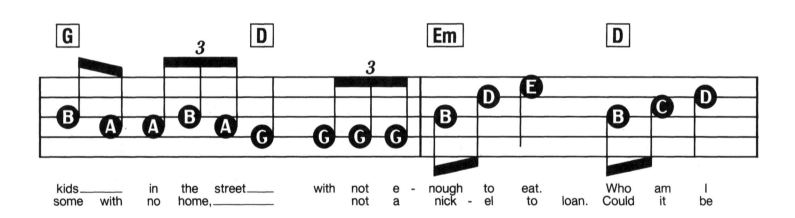

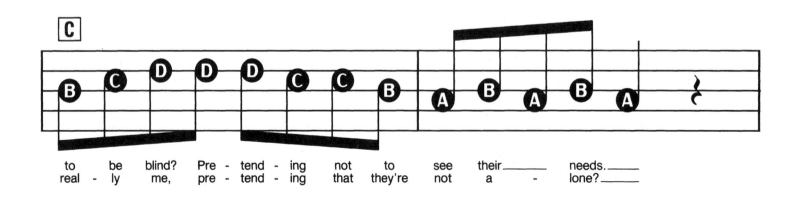

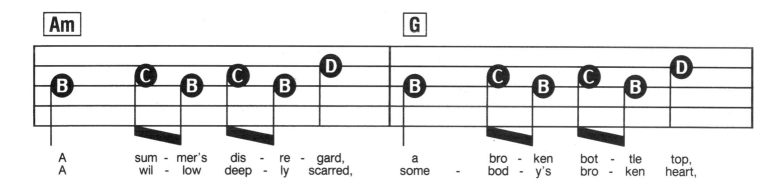

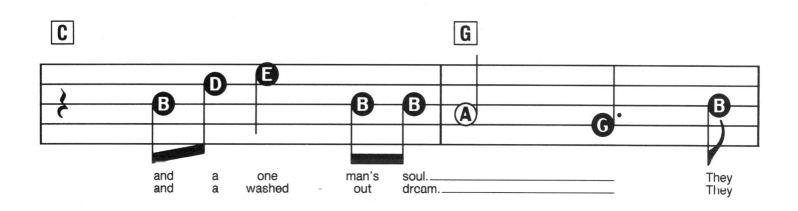

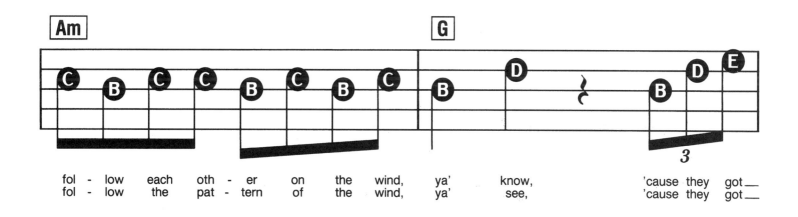

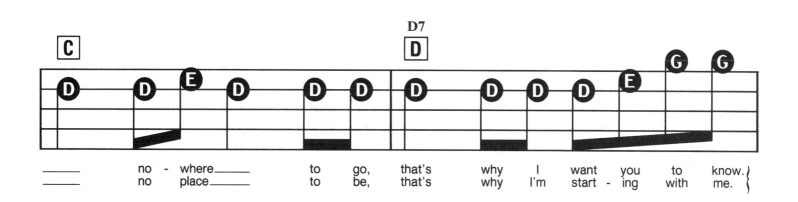

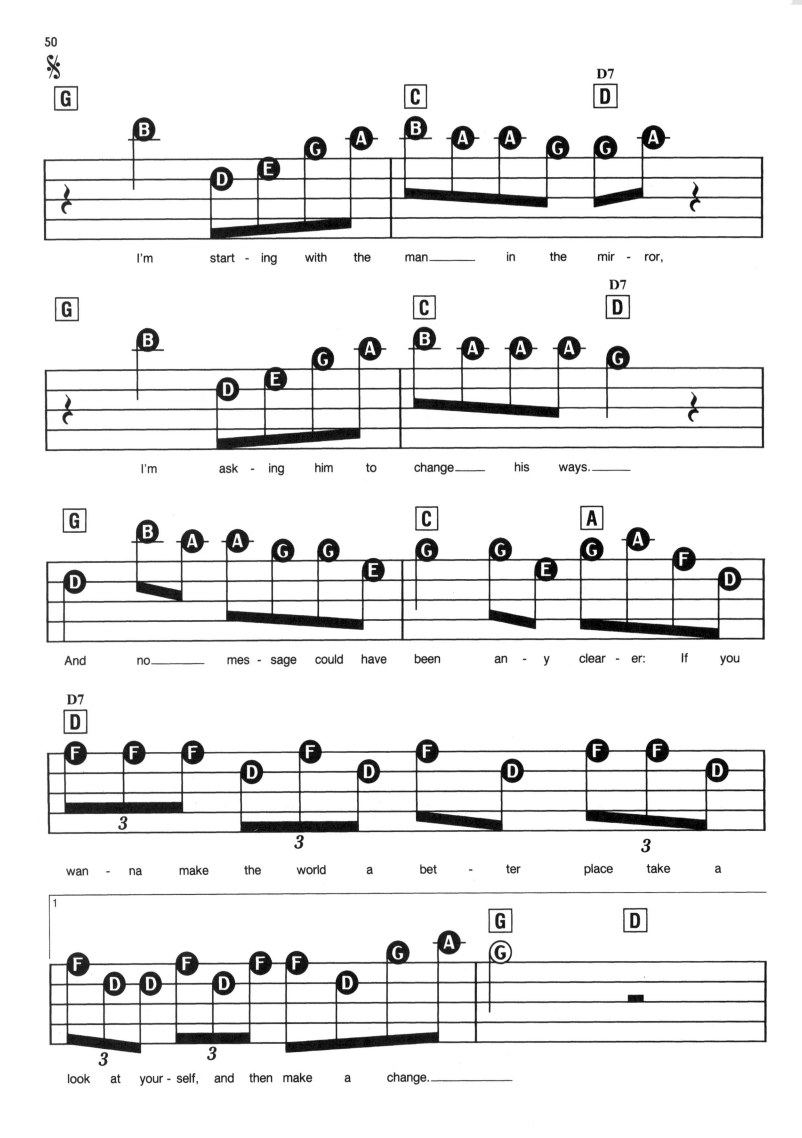

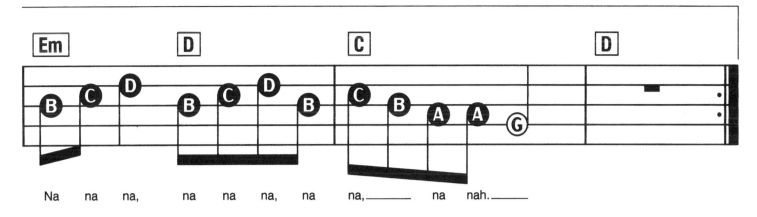

Na na na, na na na, na na,_____ na nah._____

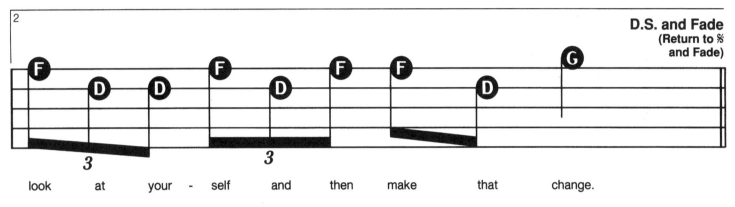

D.S. and Fade
(Return to 𝄋
and Fade)

look at your-self and then make that change.

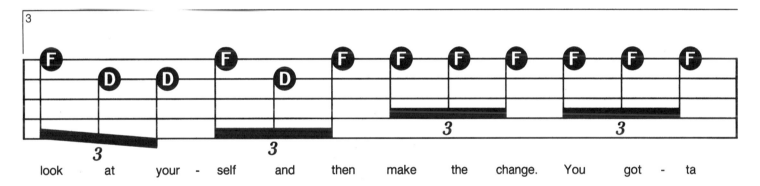

look at your-self and then make the change. You got-ta

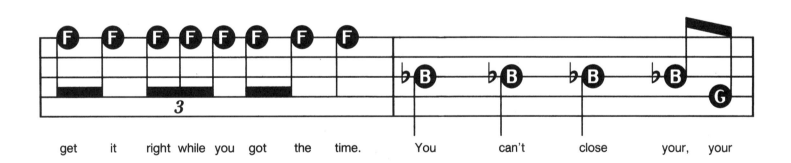

get it right while you got the time. You can't close your, your

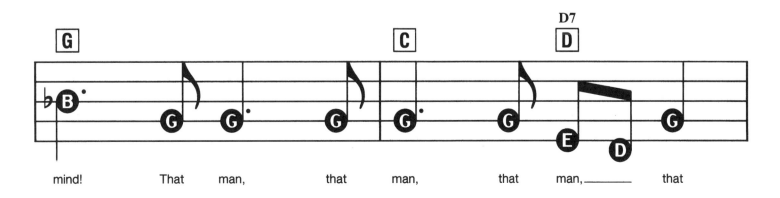

mind! That man, that man, that man,_____ that

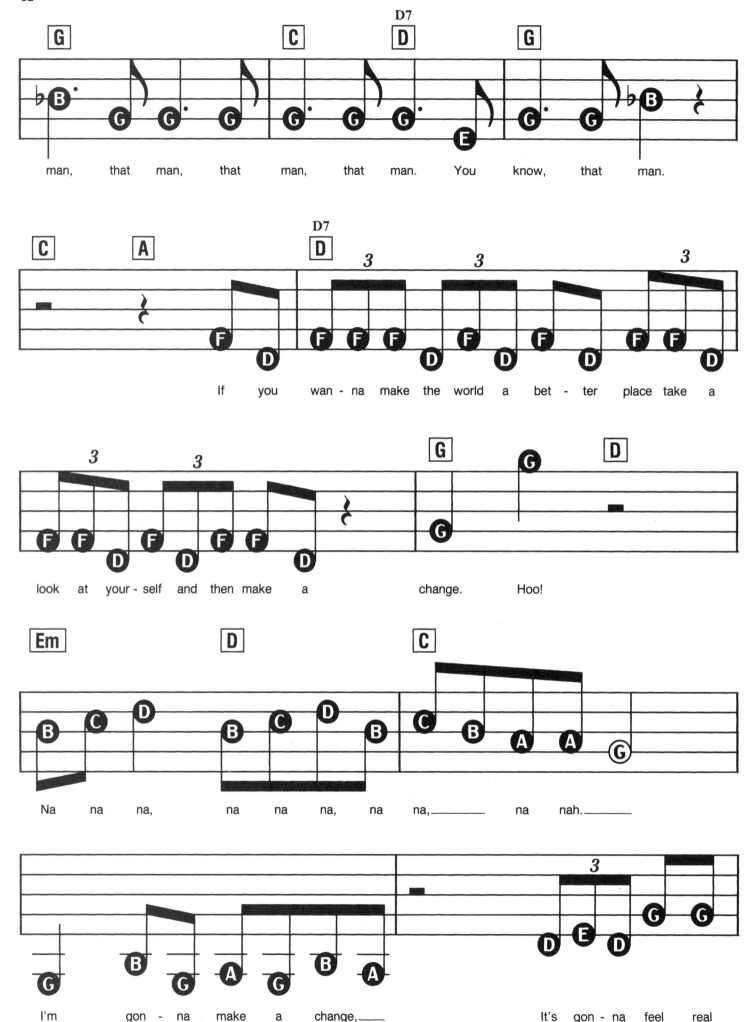

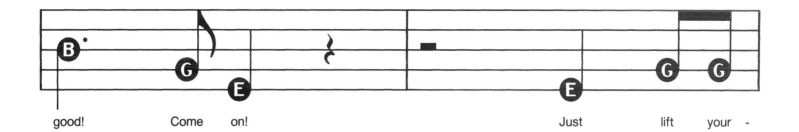

good! Come on! Just lift your -

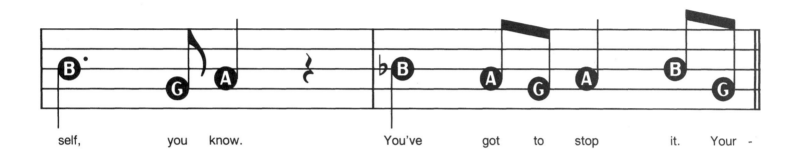

self, you know. You've got to stop it. Your -

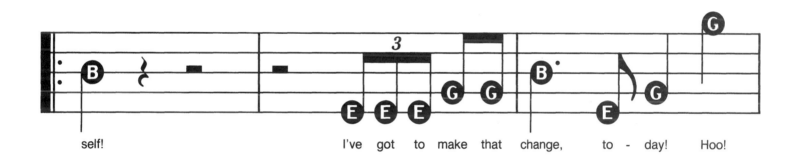

self! I've got to make that change, to - day! Hoo!

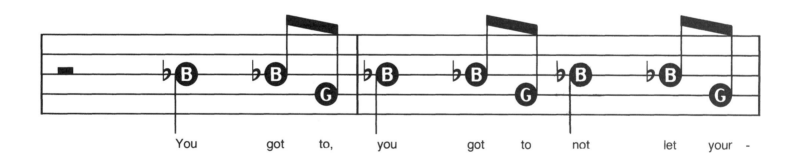

You got to, you got to not let your -

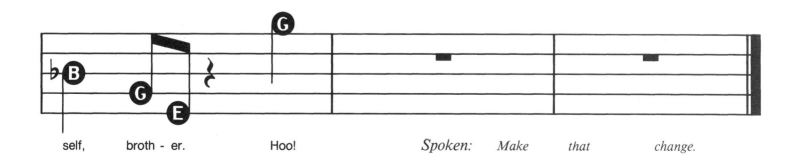

self, broth - er. Hoo! *Spoken:* *Make* *that* *change.*

Jeepers Creepers

Registration 1
Rhythm: Fox Trot or Swing

Words by Johnny Mercer
Music by Harry Warren

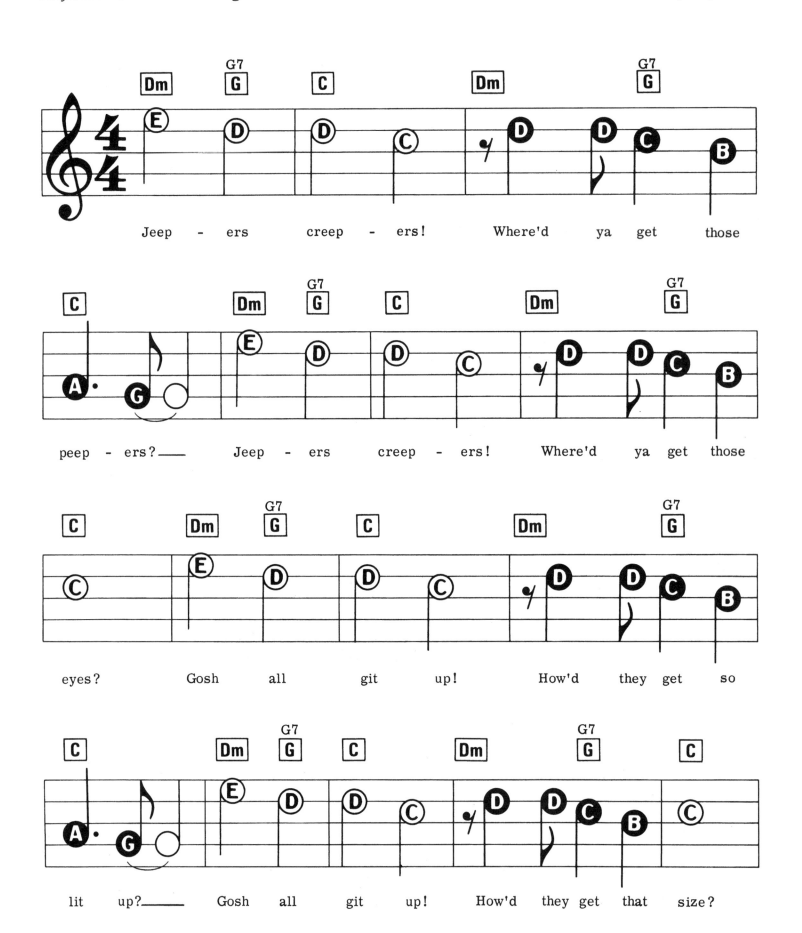

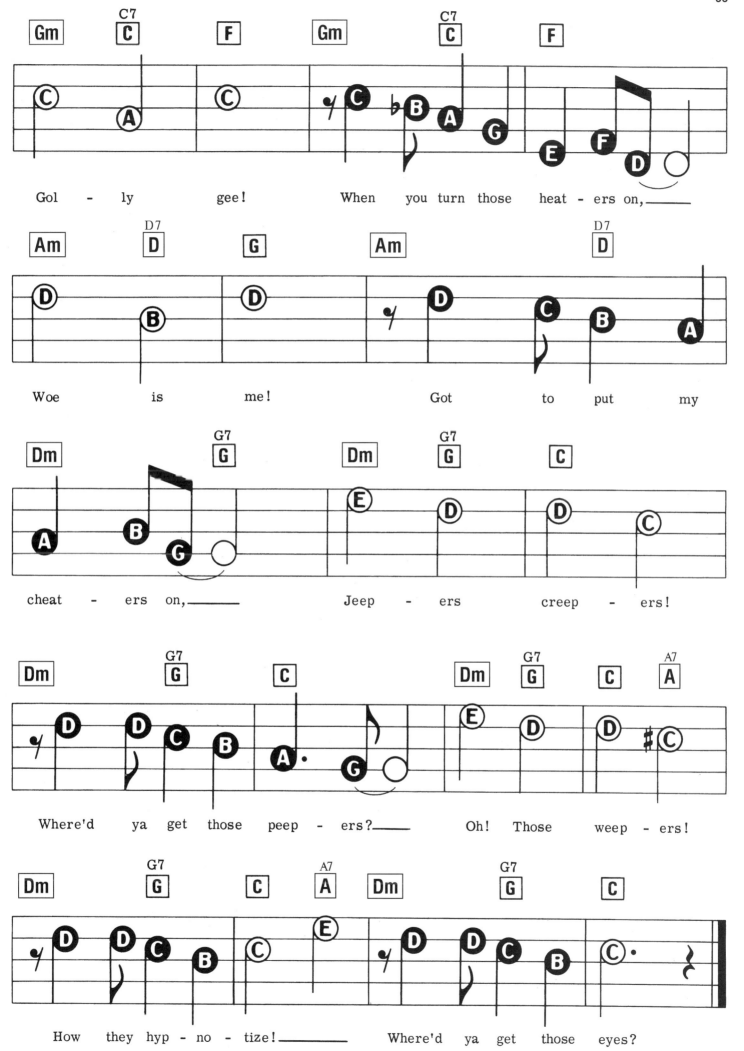

Just Friends

Registration 1
Rhythm: Swing or Fox Trot

Lyrics by Sam M. Lewis
Music by John Klenner

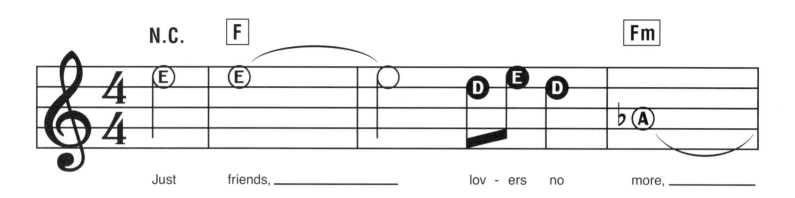

Just friends, _____ lov - ers no more, _____

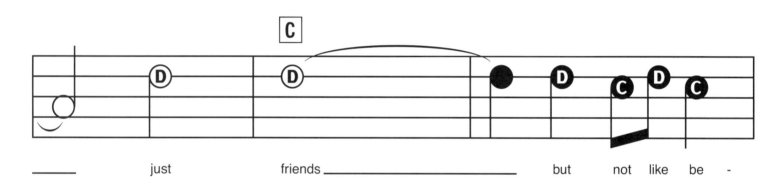

_____ just friends _____ but not like be -

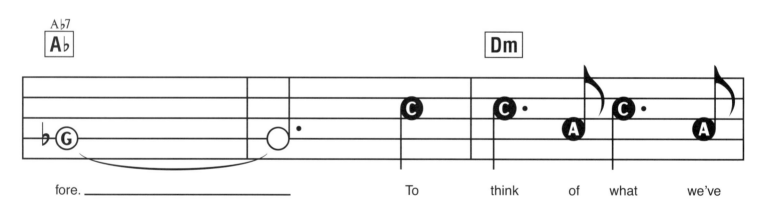

fore. _____ To think of what we've

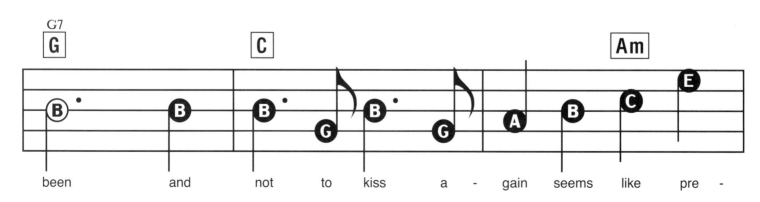

been and not to kiss a - gain seems like pre -

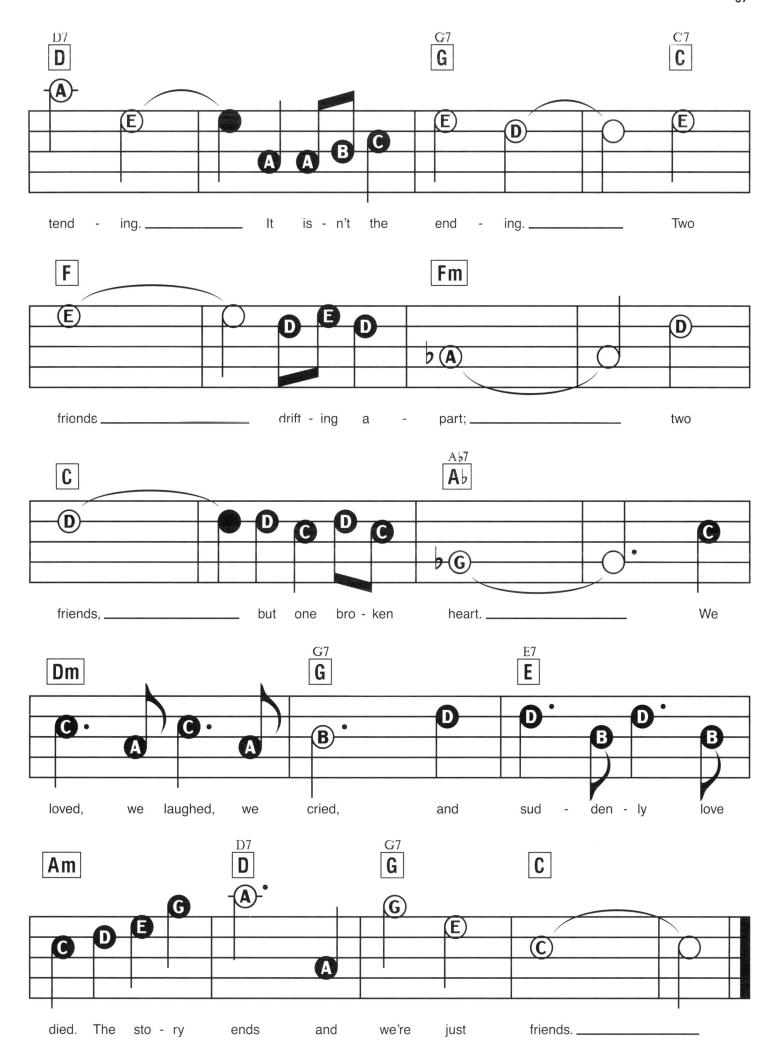

57

A Kiss to Build a Dream On

Registration 8
Rhythm: Swing or Fox Trot

Words and Music by Bert Kalmar,
Harry Ruby and Oscar Hammerstein II

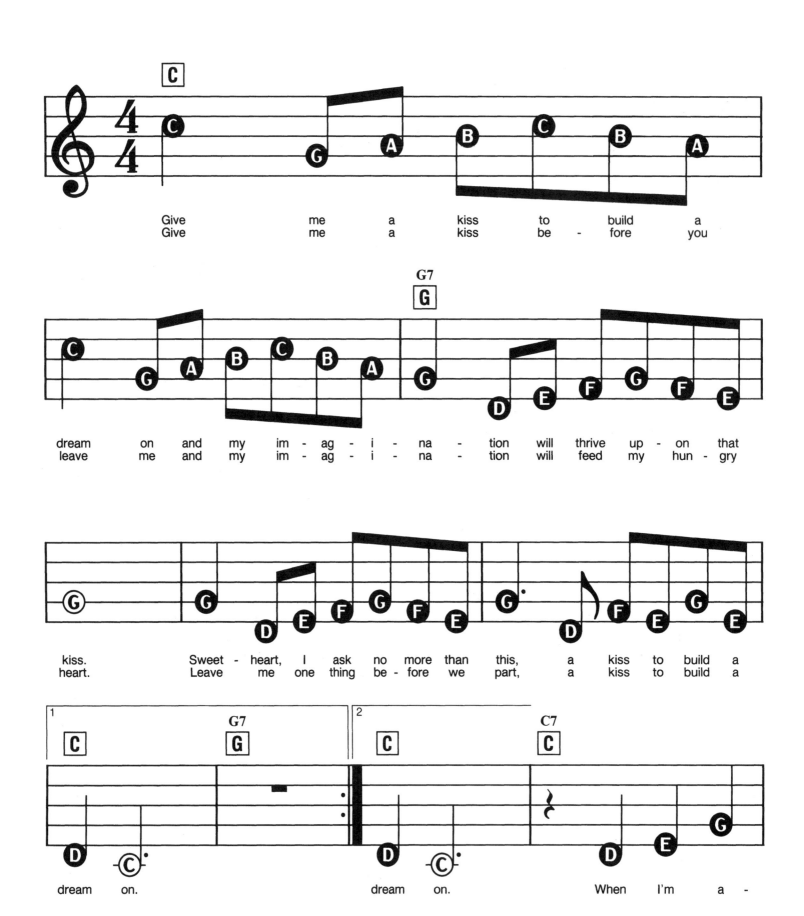

59

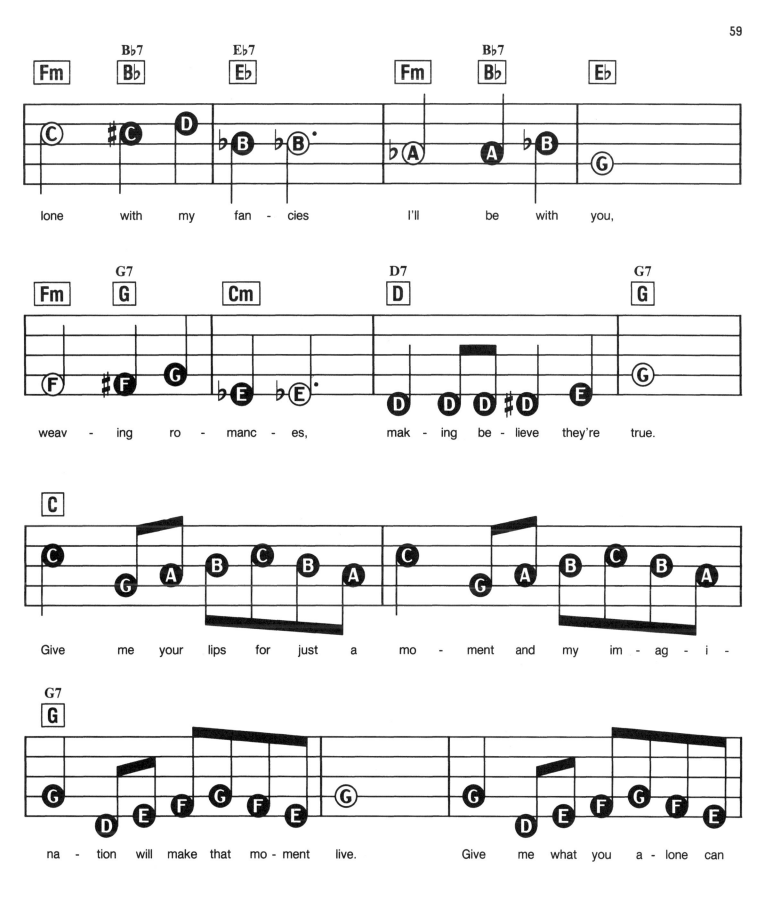
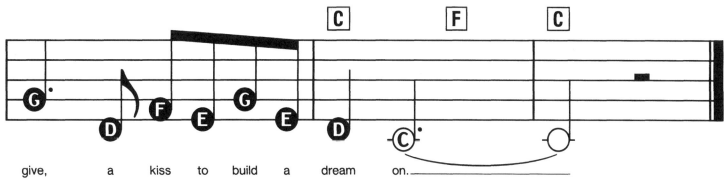

Knockin' on Heaven's Door

Registration 4
Rhythm: 8-Beat or Rock

Words and Music by
Bob Dylan

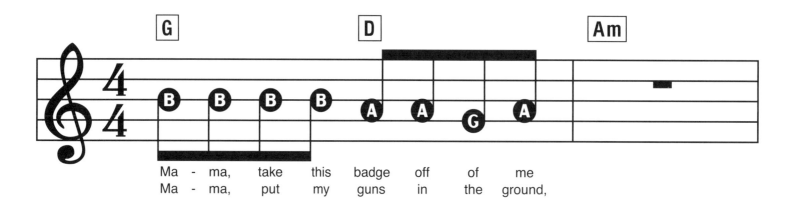

Ma - ma, take this badge off of me
Ma - ma, put my guns in the ground,

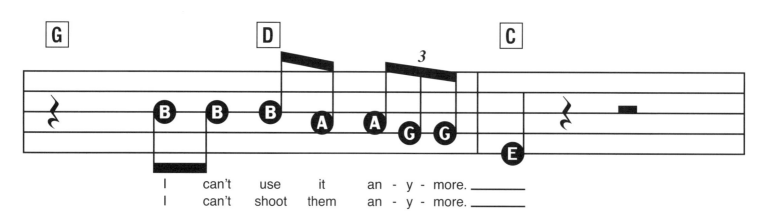

I can't use it an - y - more. _____
I can't shoot them an - y - more. _____

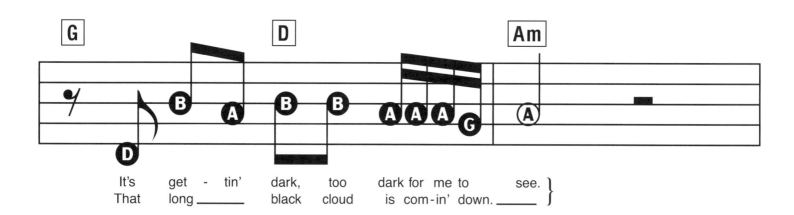

It's get - tin' dark, too dark for me to see. }
That long _____ black cloud is com - in' down. _____ }

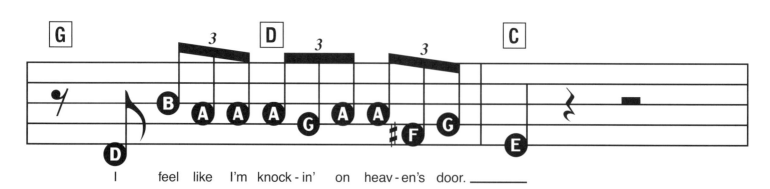

I feel like I'm knock - in' on heav - en's door. _____

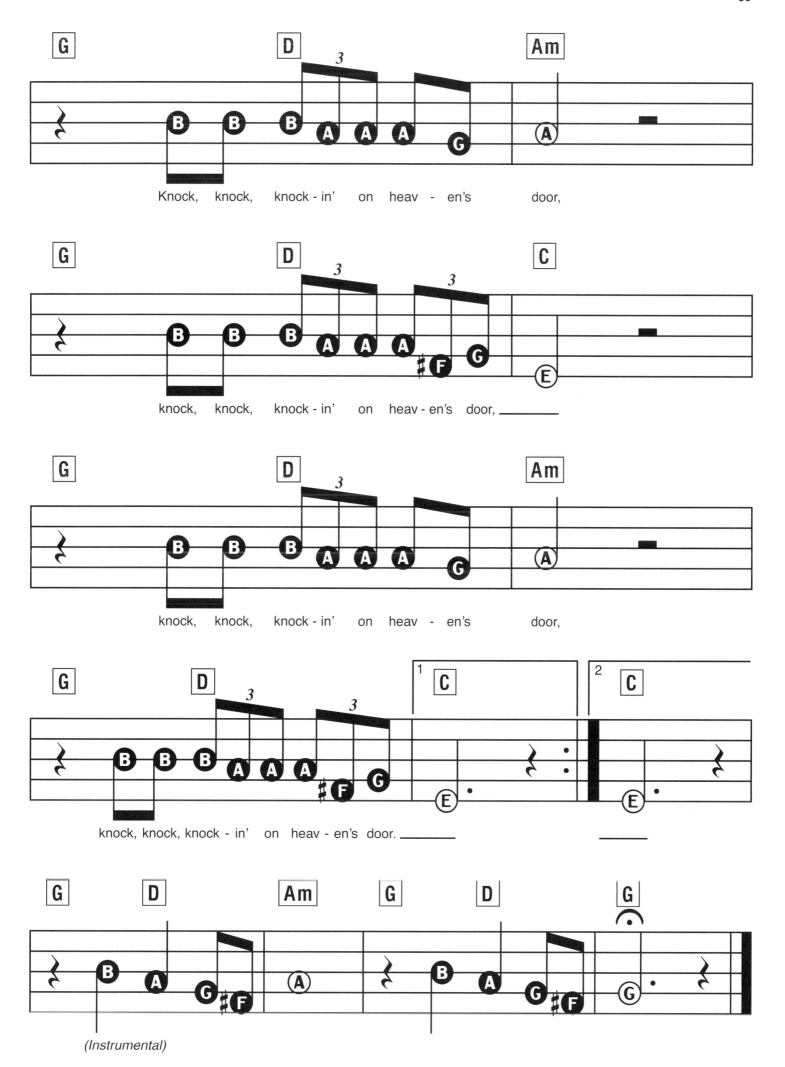

61

Moondance

Registration 2
Rhythm: Shuffle

Words and Music by
Van Morrison

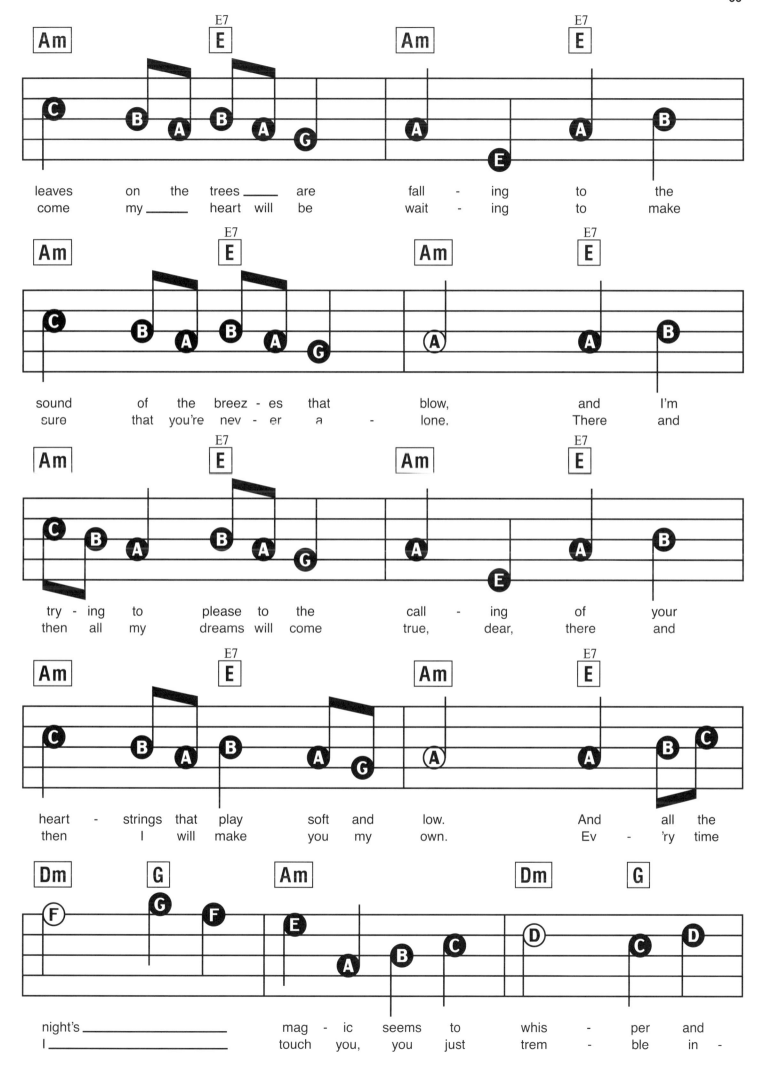

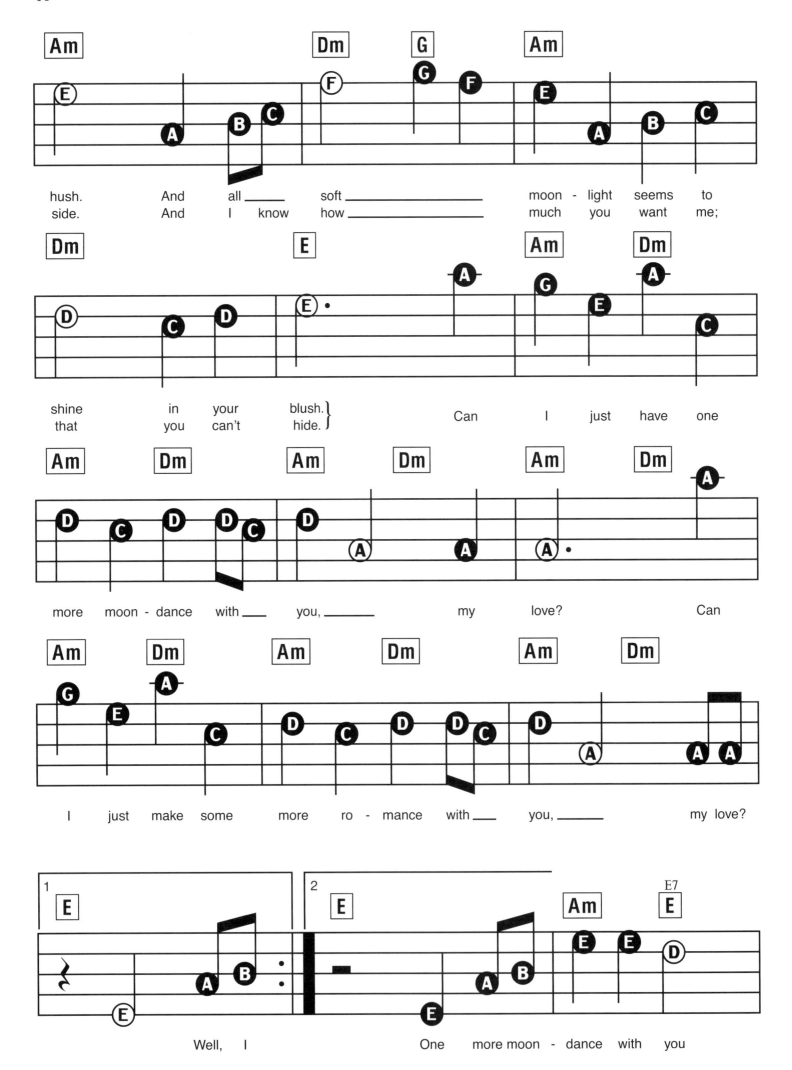

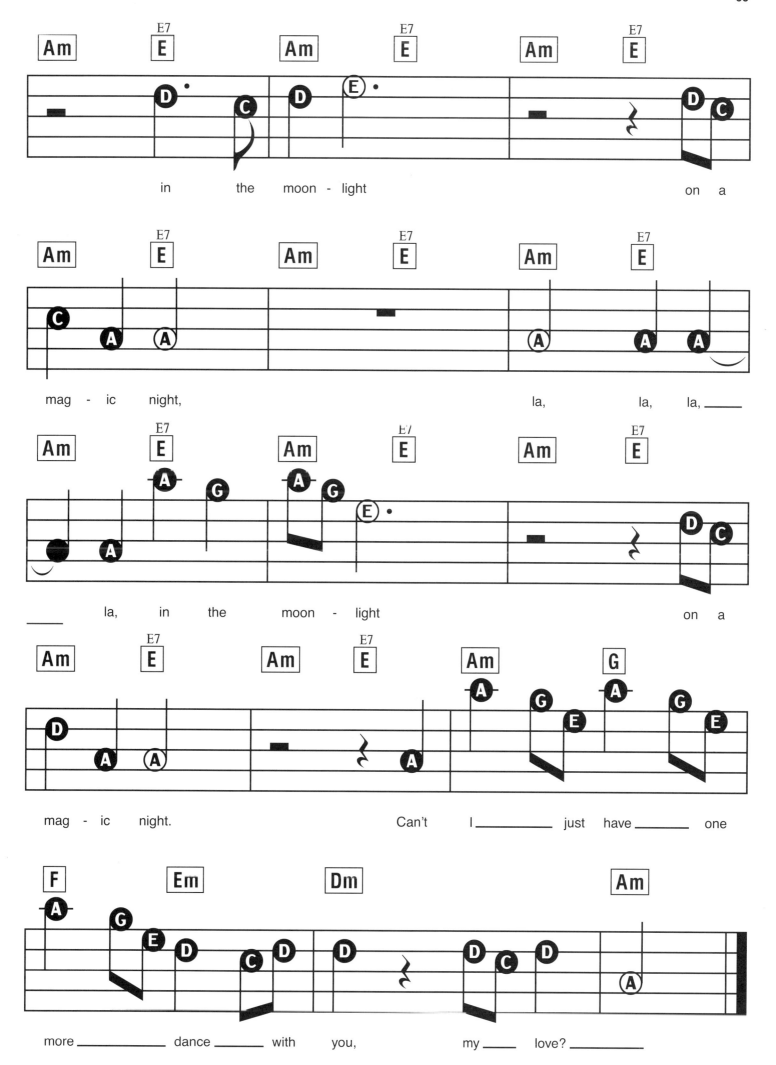

Moonlight Serenade

Registration 9
Rhythm: Swing or Big Band

Words by Mitchell Parish
Music by Glen Miller

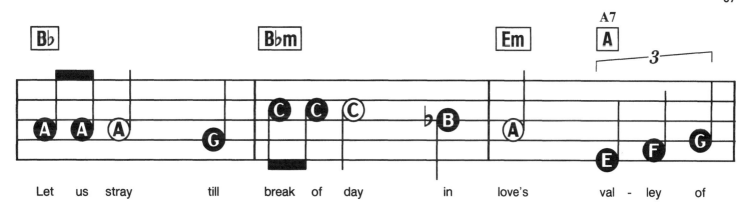

Let us stray till break of day in love's val - ley of

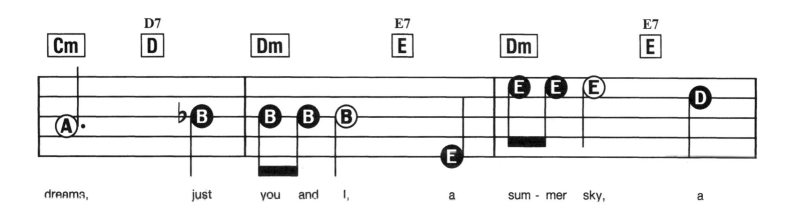

dreams, just you and I, a sum - mer sky, a

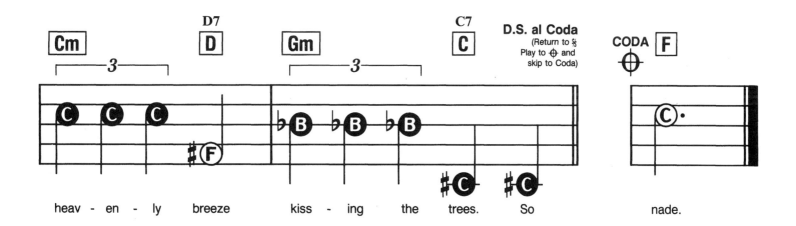

D.S. al Coda
(Return to %
Play to ⊕ and
skip to Coda)

CODA

heav - en - ly breeze kiss - ing the trees. So nade.

Additional Lyrics

D.S. So don't let me wait,
come to me tenderly in the June night.
I stand at your gate
and I sing you a song in the moonlight;
a love song, my darling,
a moonlight serenade.

Pennies from Heaven

Registration 2
Rhythm: Fox Trot or Swing

Words by John Burke
Music by Arthur Johnston

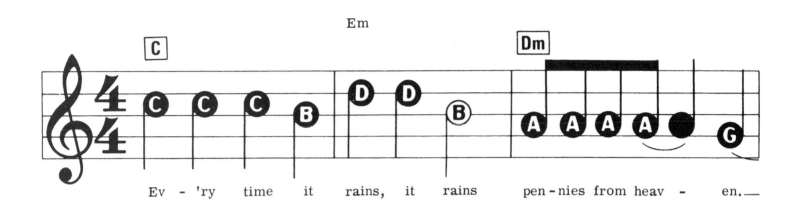

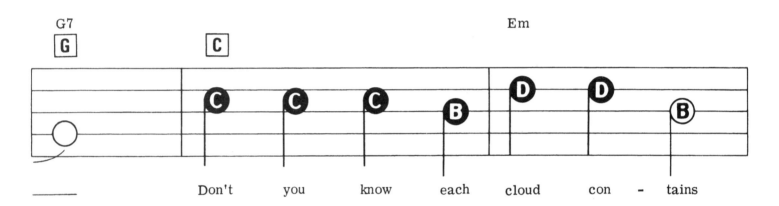

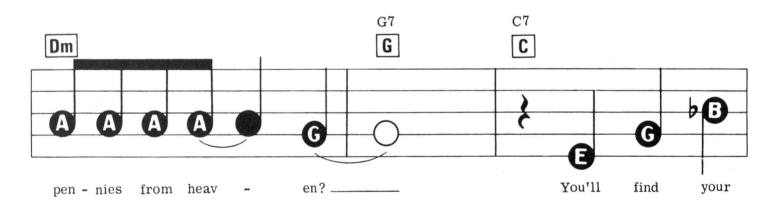

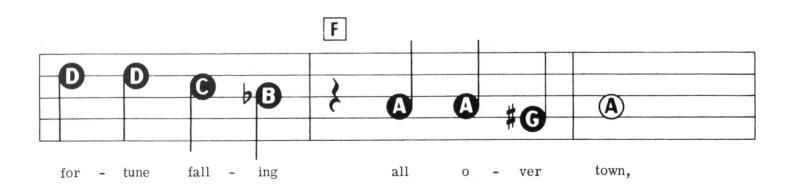

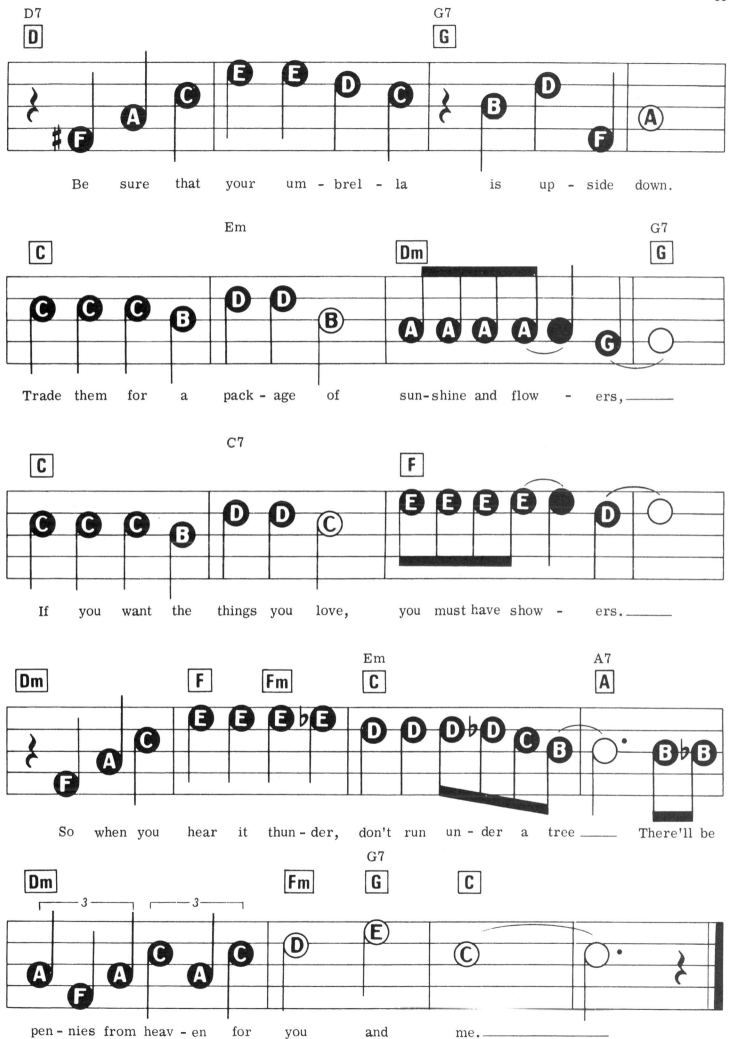

People Get Ready

Registration 1
Rhythm: 4/4 Ballad or 8-Beat

Words and Music by
Curtis Mayfield

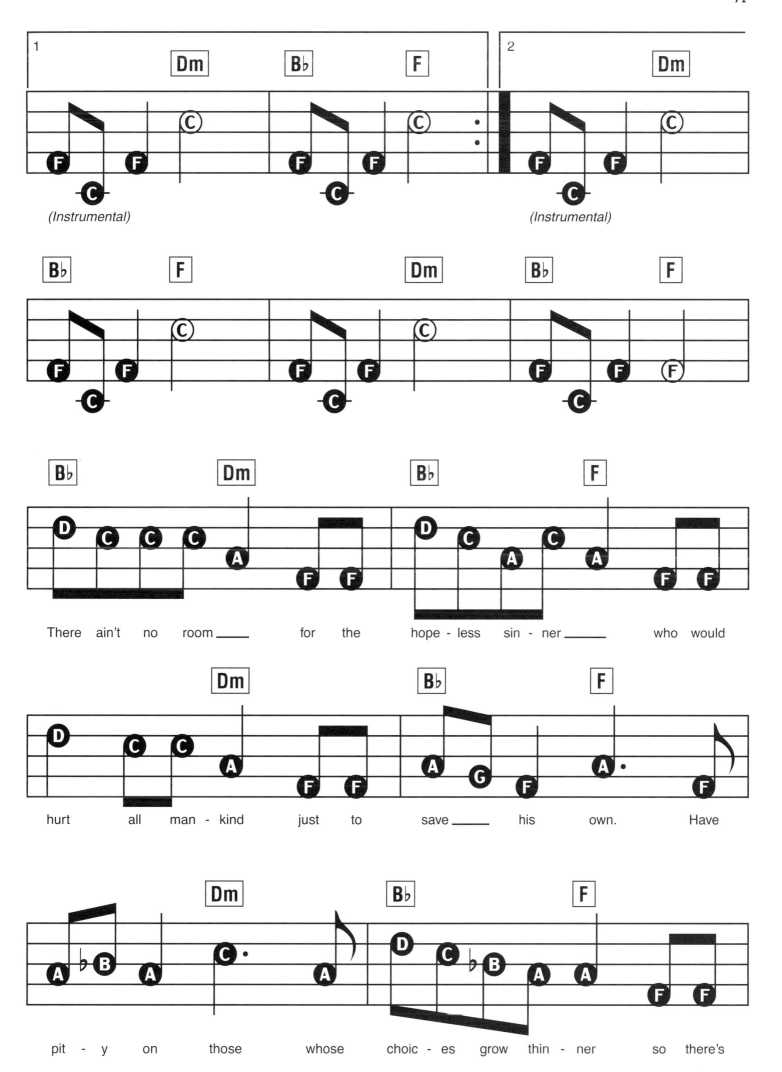

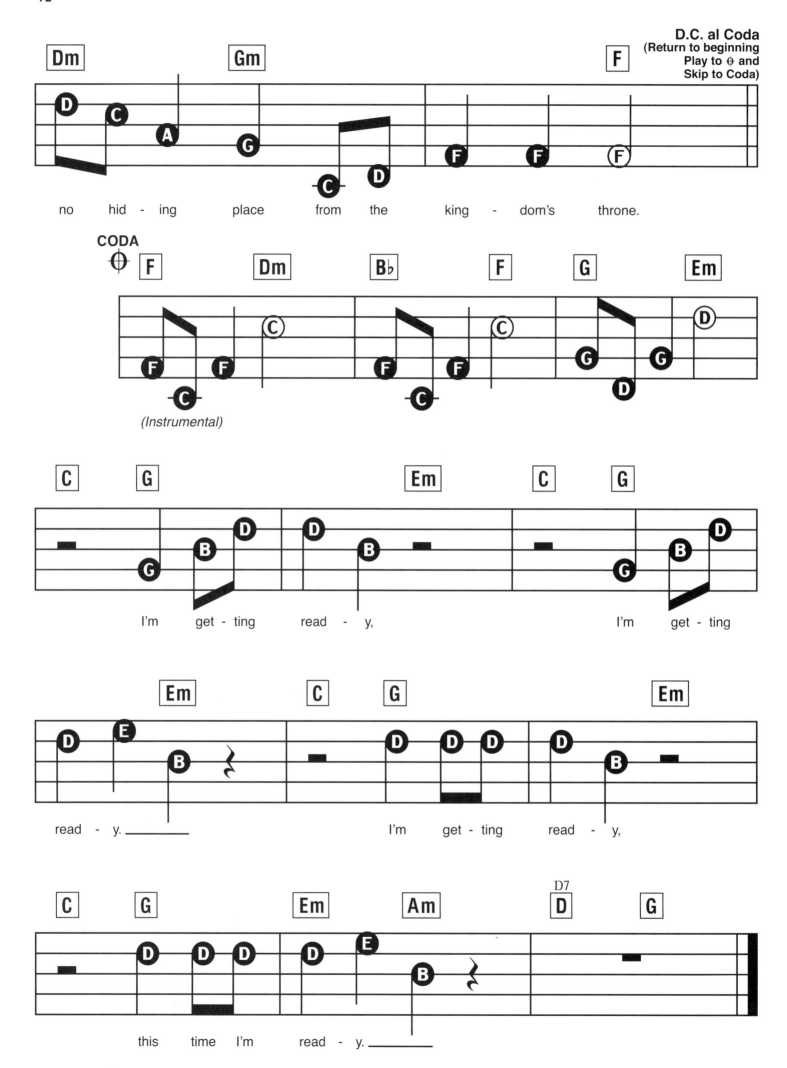

D.C. al Coda
(Return to beginning
Play to ⊕ and
Skip to Coda)

no hid - ing place from the king - dom's throne.

CODA

(Instrumental)

I'm get - ting read - y, I'm get - ting

read - y. _____ I'm get - ting read - y,

this time I'm read - y. _____

That's All

Registration 10
Rhythm: Ballad

Words and Music by Bob Haymes
and Alan E. Brandt

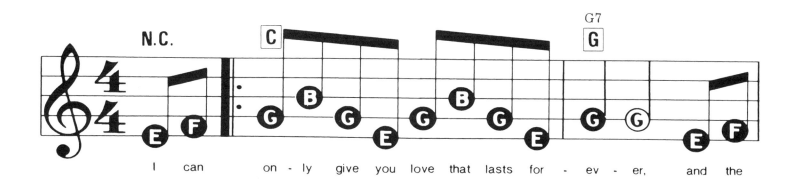

I can on-ly give you love that lasts for-ev-er, and the

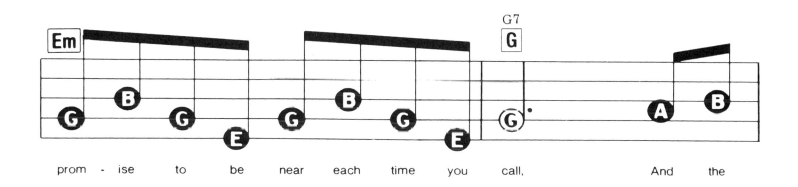

prom-ise to be near each time you call, And the

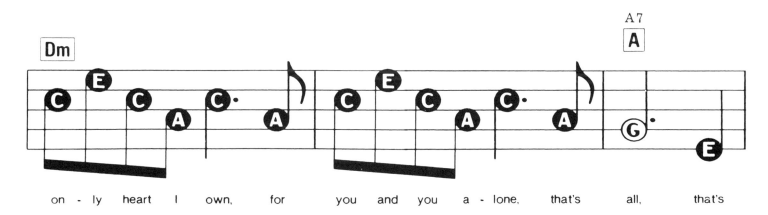

on-ly heart I own, for you and you a-lone, that's all, that's

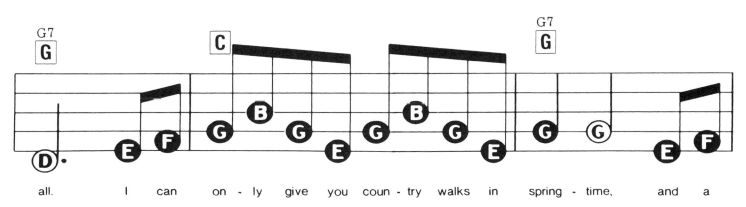

all. I can on-ly give you coun-try walks in spring-time, and a

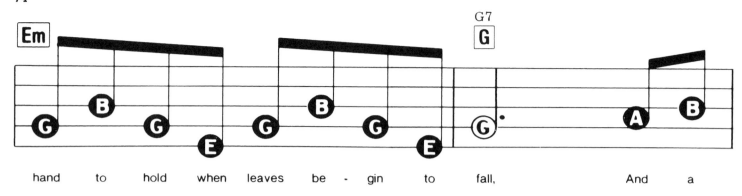

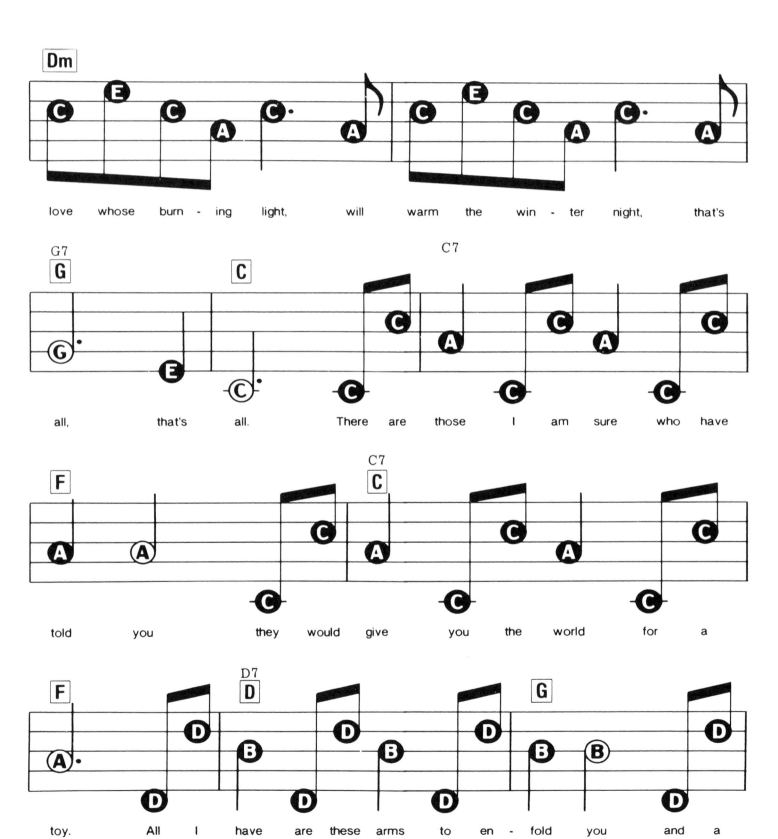

75

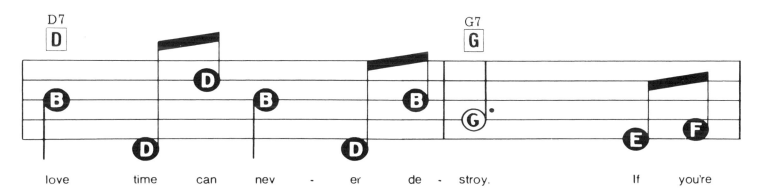

love time can nev - er de - stroy. If you're

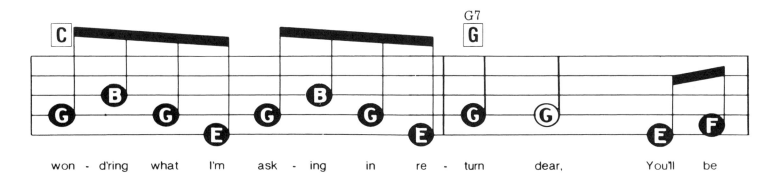

won - d'ring what I'm ask - ing in re - turn dear, You'll be

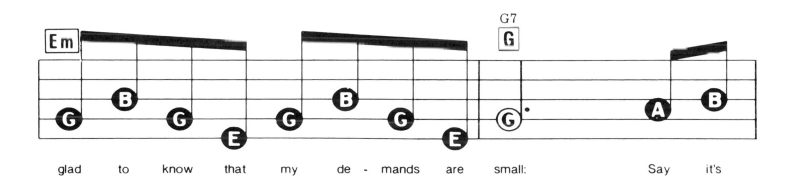

glad to know that my de - mands are small: Say it's

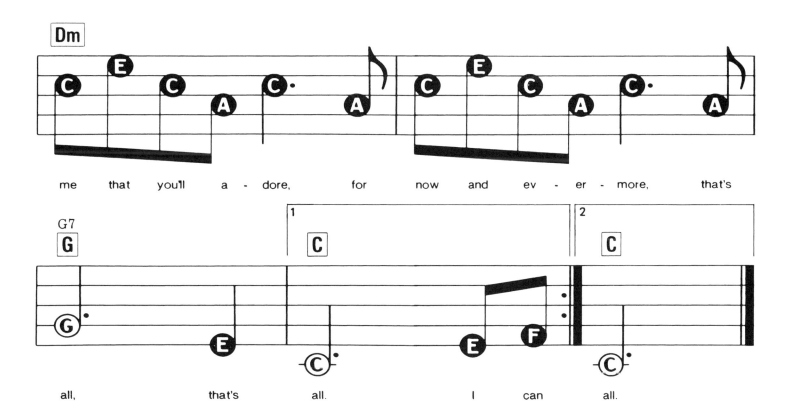

me that you'll a - dore, for now and ev - er - more, that's

all, that's all. I can all.

The River Seine
(La Seine)

Registration 2
Rhythm: Waltz

Words and Music by Allan Roberts and Alan Holt
Original French Text by Flavien Monod and Guy LaFarge

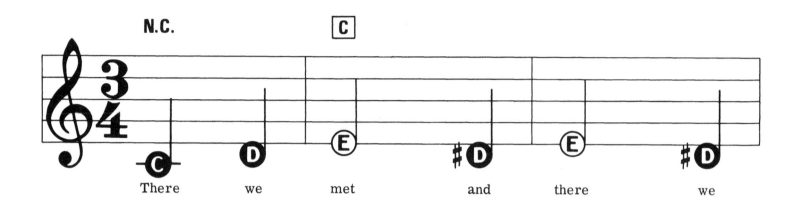

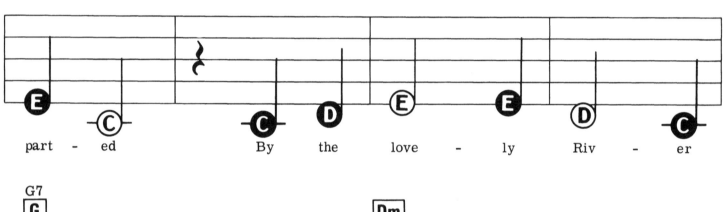

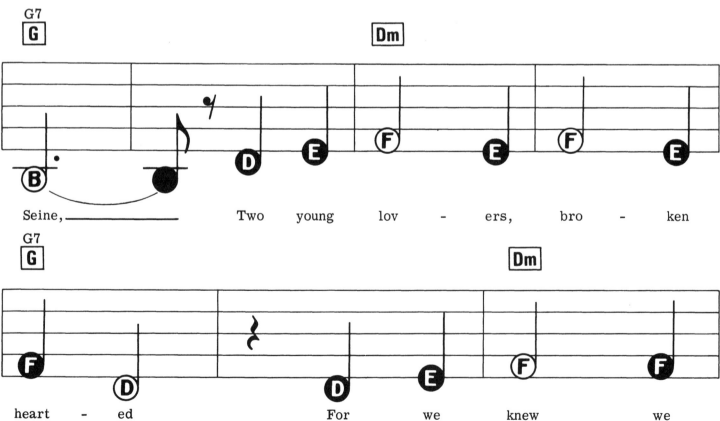

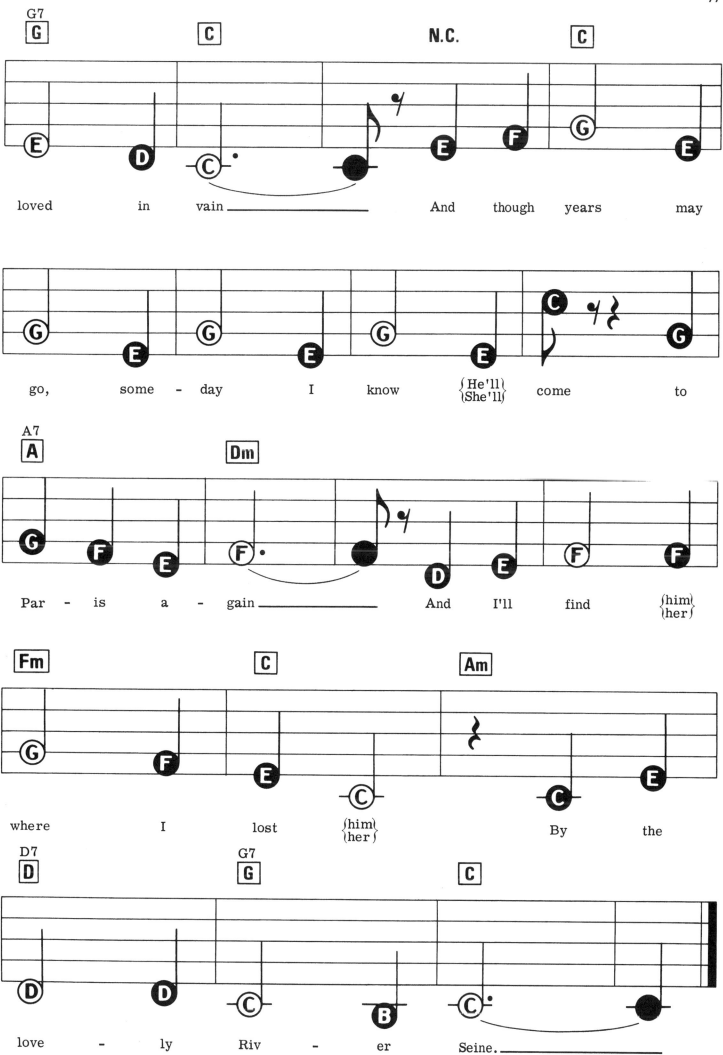

Ruby

Registration 2
Rhythm: Swing

Music by Heinz Roemheld
Words by Mitchell Parish

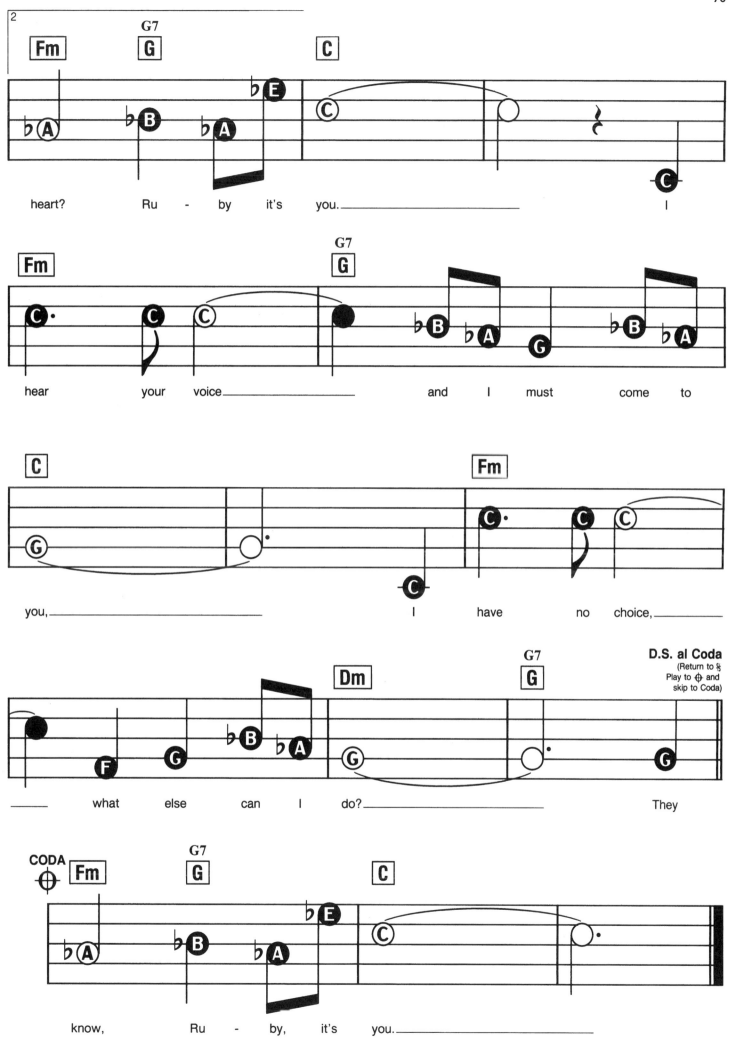

Singin' in the Rain

Registration 4
Rhythm: Swing

Lyric by Arthur Freed
Music by Nacio Herb Brown

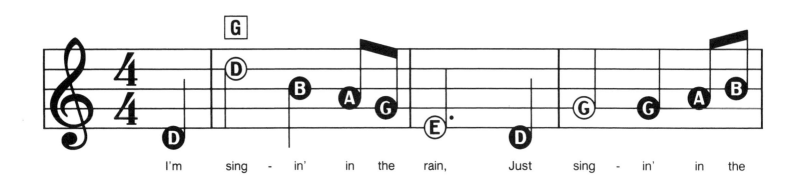

I'm sing - in' in the rain, Just sing - in' in the

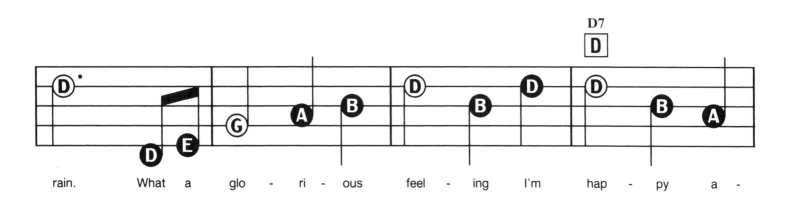

rain. What a glo - ri - ous feel - ing I'm hap - py a -

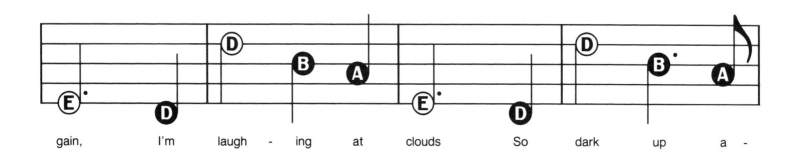

gain, I'm laugh - ing at clouds So dark up a -

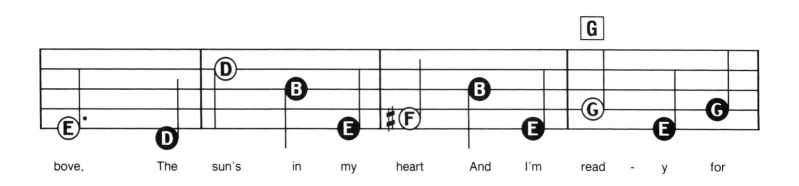

bove, The sun's in my heart And I'm read - y for

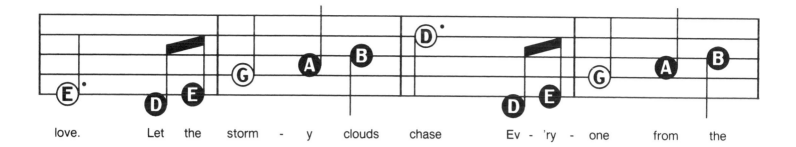

love. Let the storm - y clouds chase Ev - 'ry - one from the

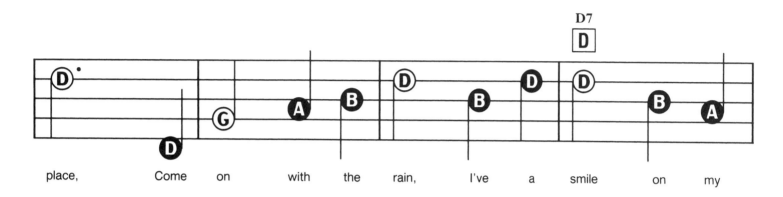

place, Come on with the rain, I've a smile on my

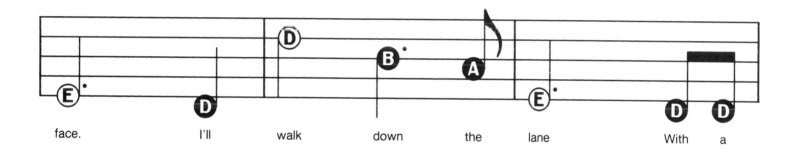

face. I'll walk down the lane With a

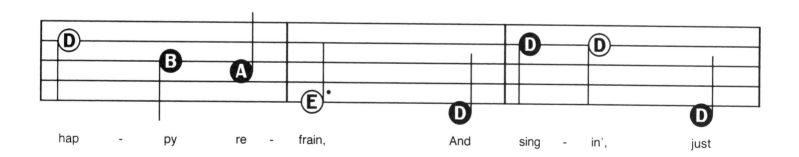

hap - py re - frain, And sing - in', just

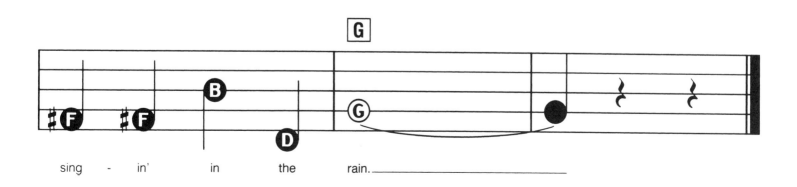

sing - in' in the rain.

Street of Dreams

Registration 1
Rhythm: Ballad or Fox Trot

Words and Music by Sam M. Lewis
and Victor Young

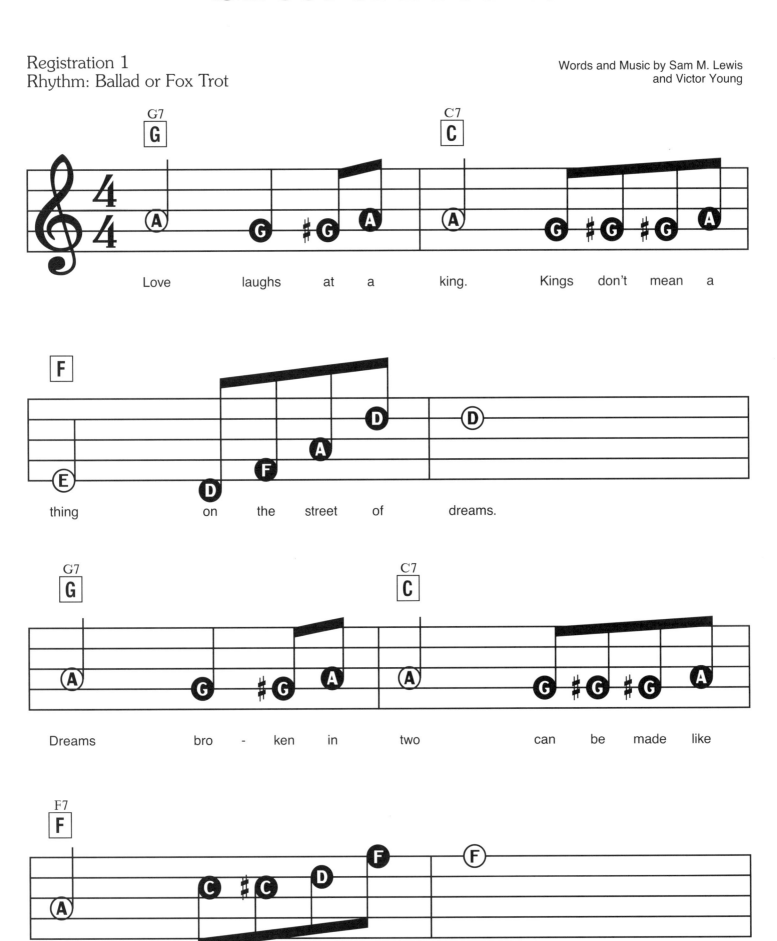

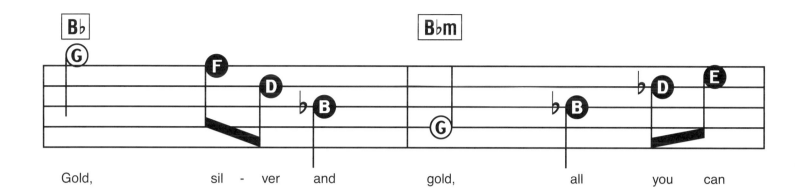

Gold, sil - ver and gold, all you can

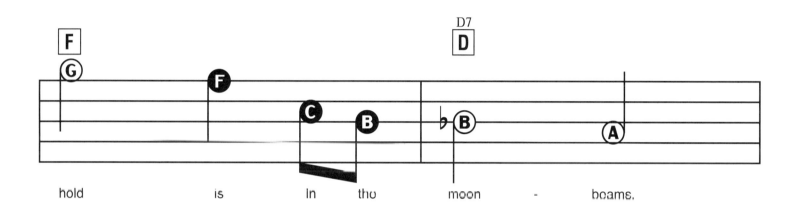

hold is In the moon - beams.

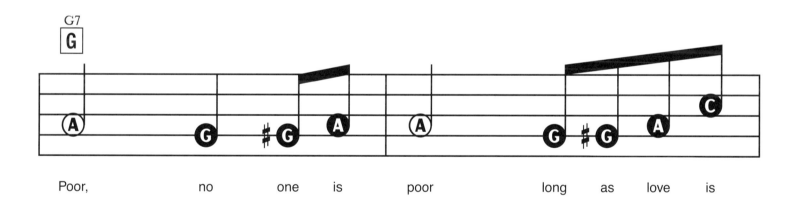

Poor, no one is poor long as love is

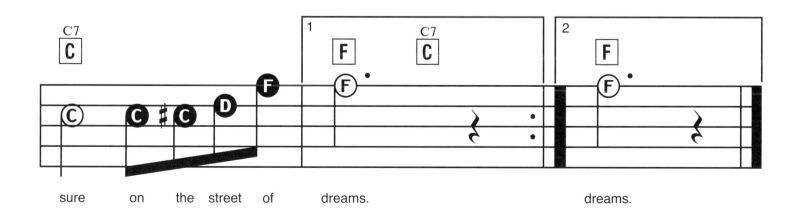

sure on the street of dreams. dreams.

Sunny

Registration: 3
Rhythm: Fox Trot or Ballad

Words and Music by
Bobby Hebb

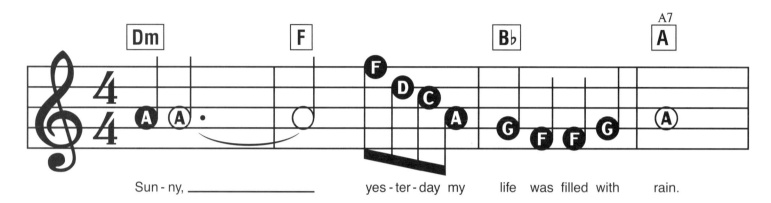

Sun - ny, _____ yes - ter - day my life was filled with rain.

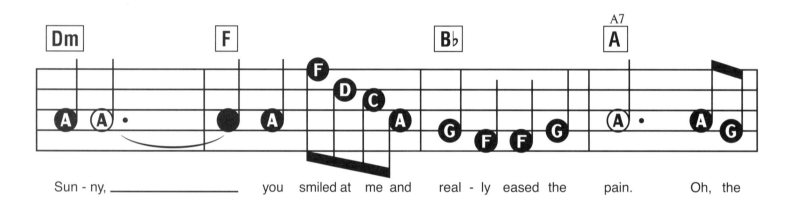

Sun - ny, _____ you smiled at me and real - ly eased the pain. Oh, the

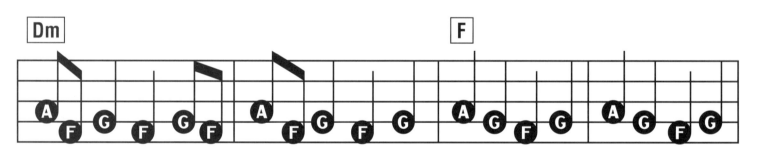

dark days are gone and the bright days are here. My Sun - ny one shines so sin - cere. Oh,

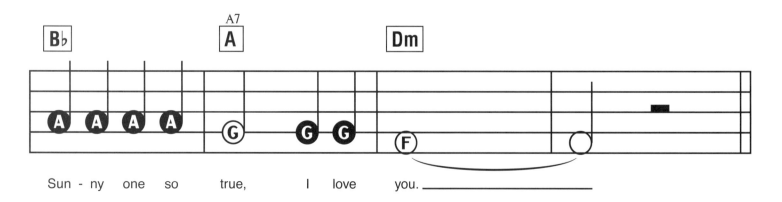

Sun - ny one so true, I love you. _____

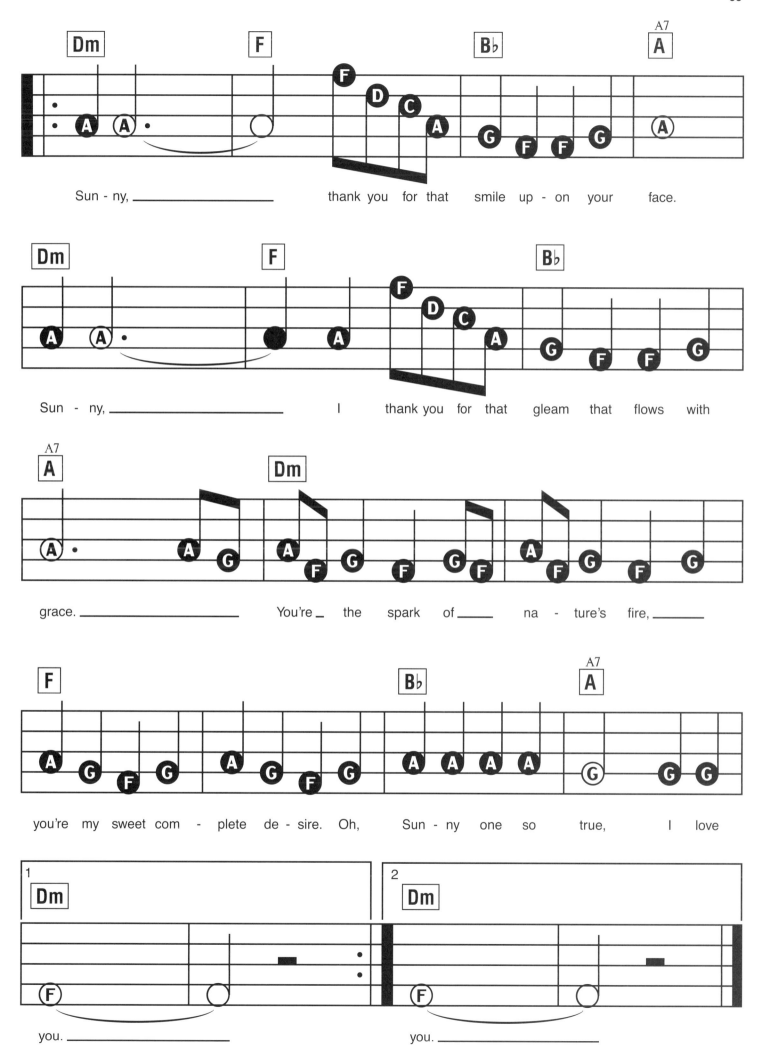

Taking a Chance on Love

Registration 7
Rhythm: Fox Trot or Swing

Words by John La Touche and Ted Fetter
Music by Vernon Duke

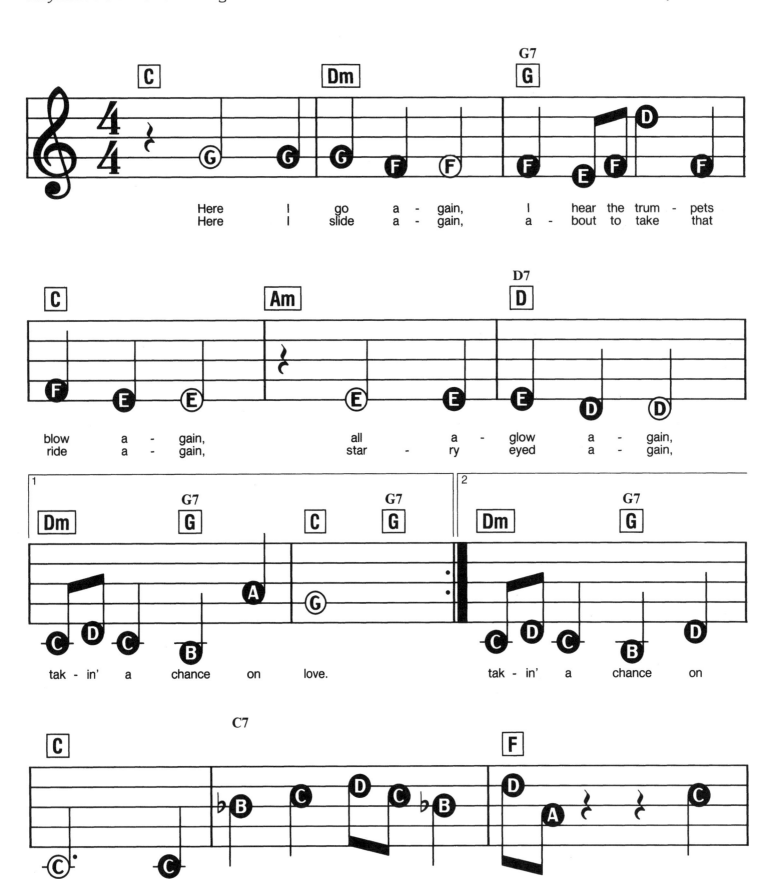

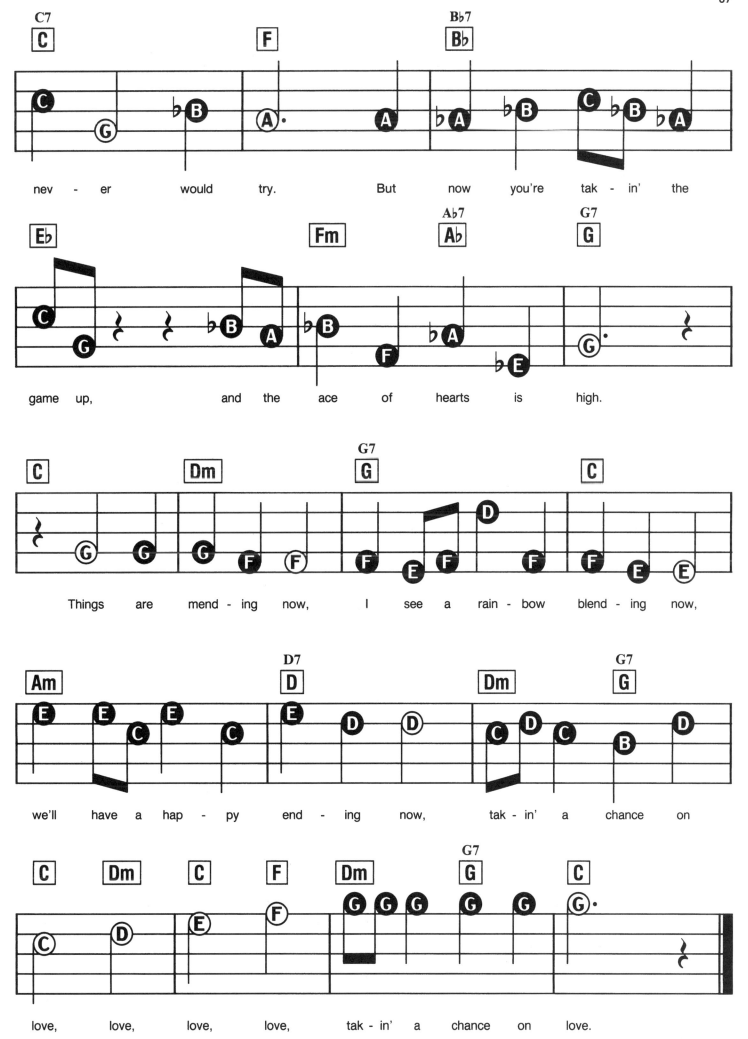

A Time for Love

Registration 7
Rhythm: Swing or Jazz

Music by Johnny Mandel
Words by Paul Francis Webster

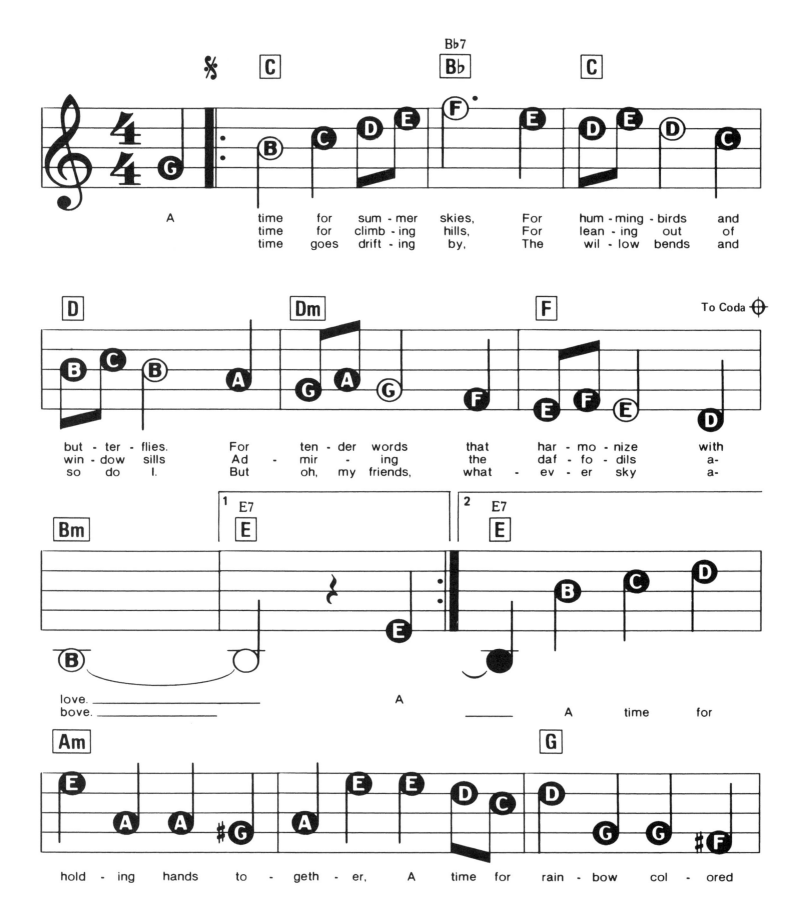

89

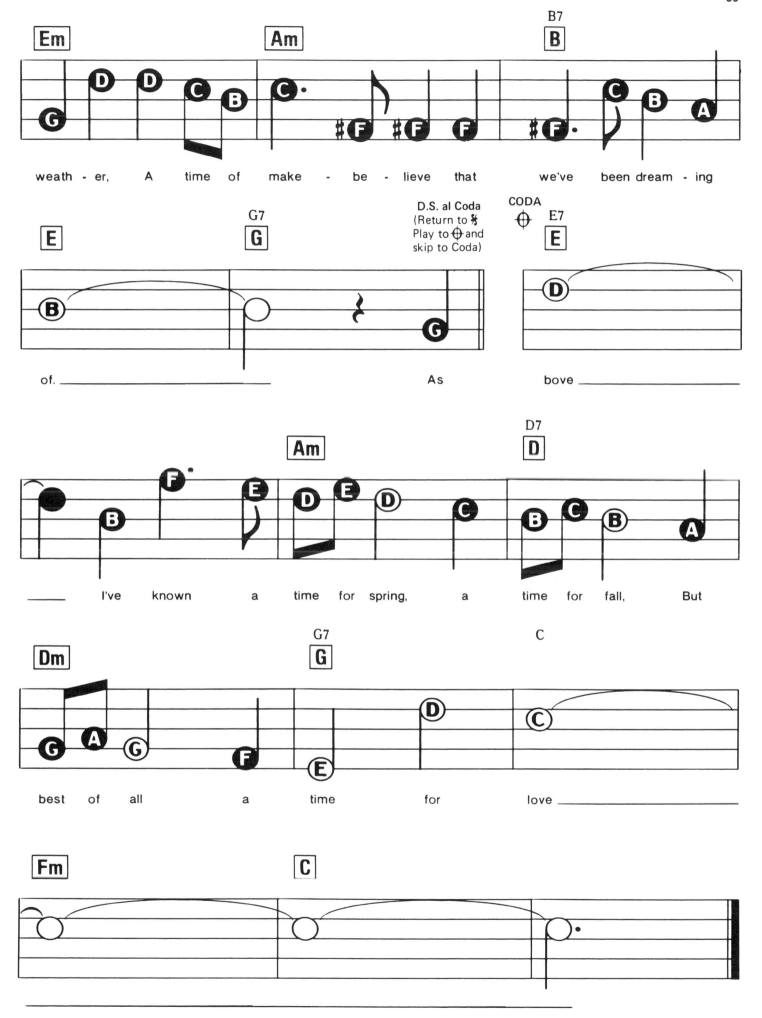

Tip-Toe Thru' the Tulips with Me

Registration 2
Rhythm: Swing or Jazz

Words by Al Dubin
Music by Joe Burke

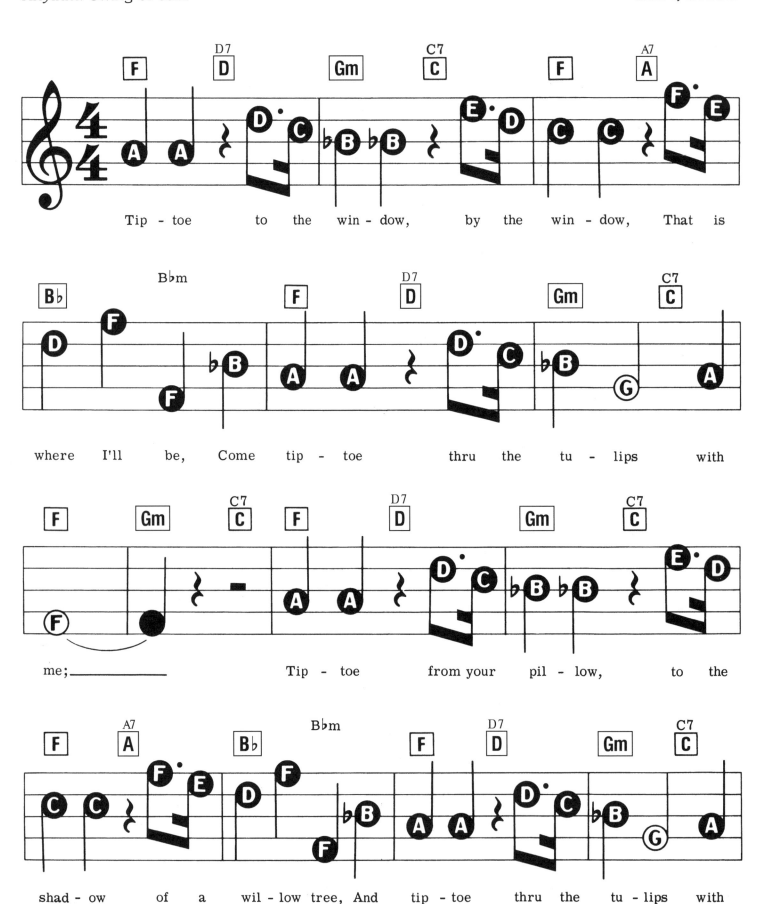

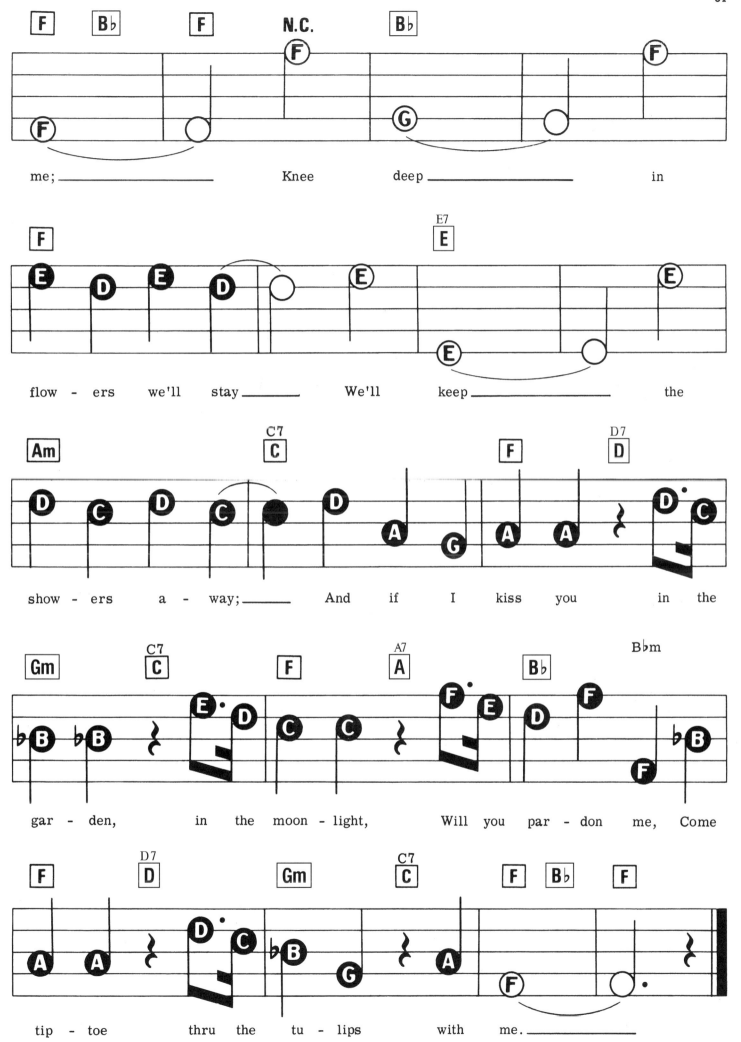

Walk On By

Registration 4
Rhythm: Rock, Pops, or Bossa Nova

Lyric by Hal David
Music by Burt Bacharach

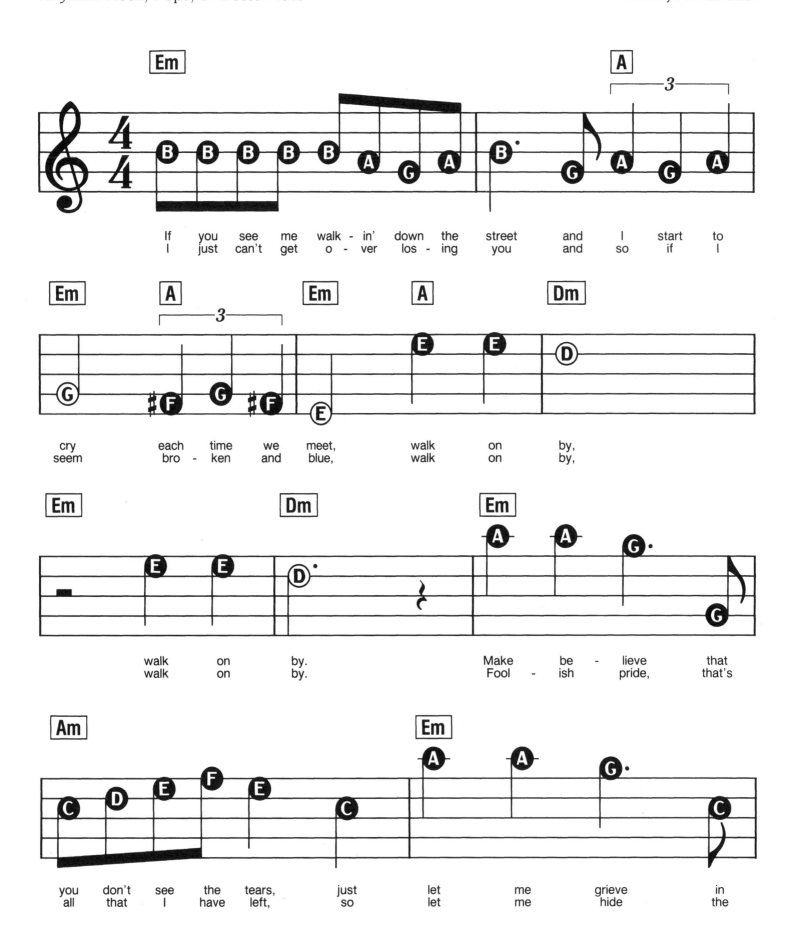

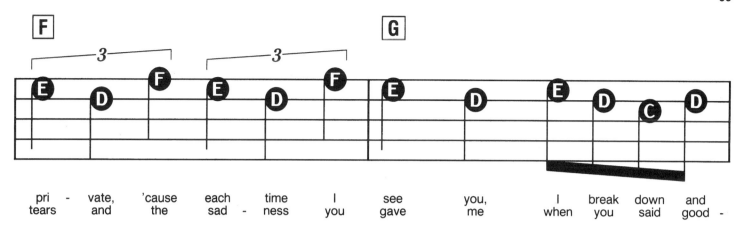

pri - vate, 'cause each time I see you, I break down and
tears and the sad - ness you gave me when you said good -

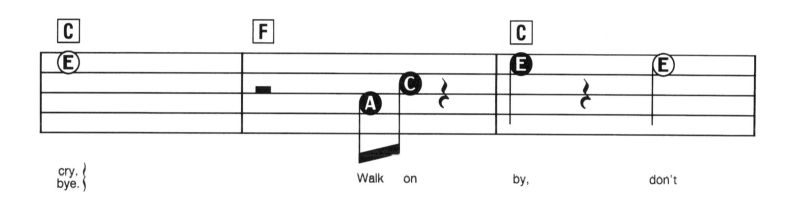

cry.
bye.
Walk on by, don't

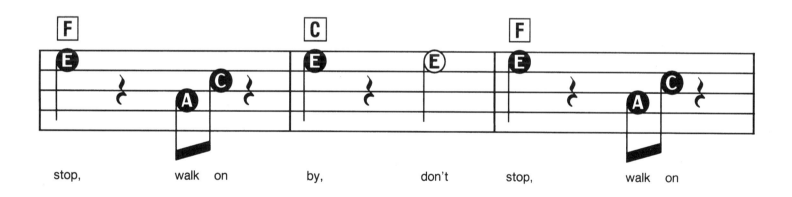

stop, walk on by, don't stop, walk on

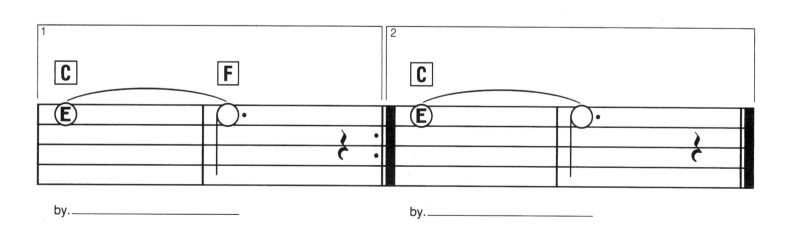

by._____ by._____

We're in This Love Together

Registration 4
Rhythm: Swing or Shuffle

Words and Music by Keith Stegall
and Roger Murrah

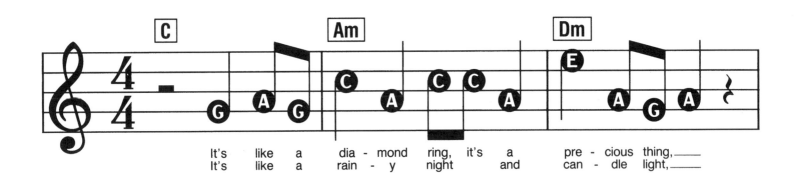

It's like a dia - mond ring, it's a pre - cious thing,____
It's like a rain - y night and can - dle light,____

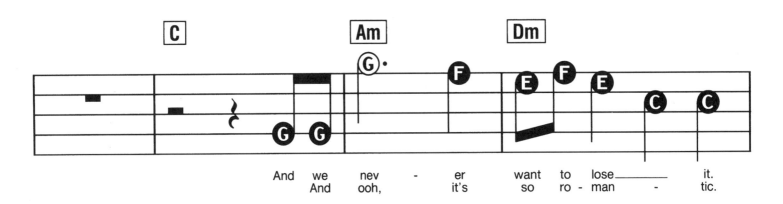

And we nev - er want to lose____ it.
And ooh, it's so ro - man - tic.

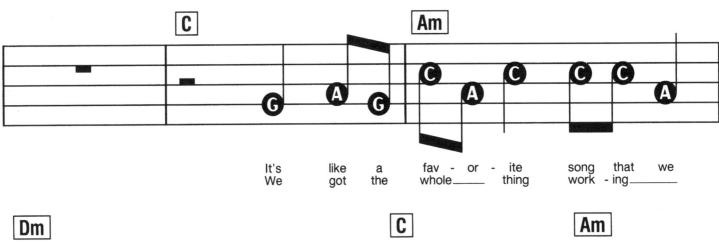

It's like a fav - or - ite song that we
We got the whole____ thing work - ing____

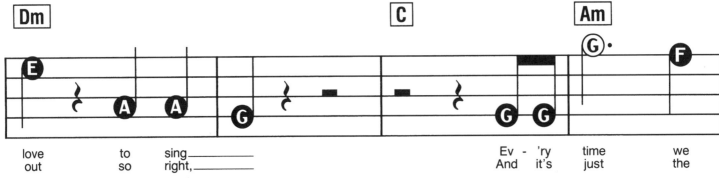

love to sing____
out so right,____
Ev - 'ry time we
And it's just the

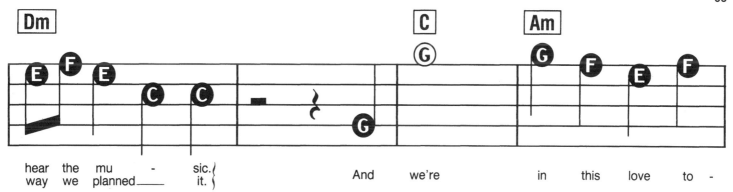

hear the mu - sic.
way we planned___ it.
And we're in this love to -

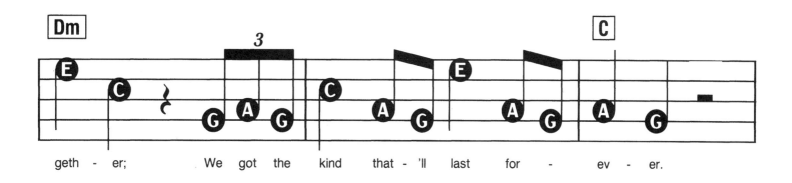

geth - er; We got the kind that - 'll last for - ev - er.

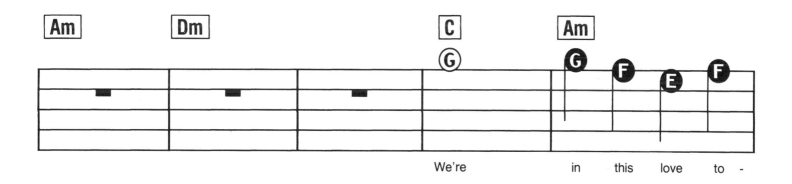

We're in this love to -

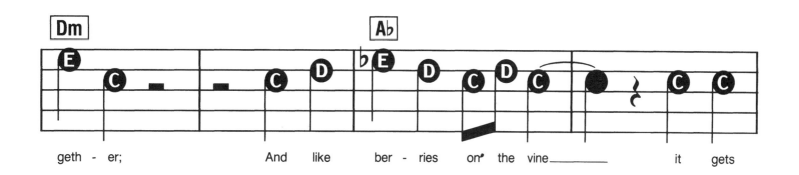

geth - er; And like ber - ries on' the vine___ it gets

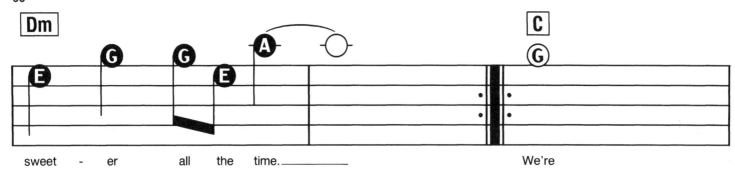

sweet - er all the time._____ We're

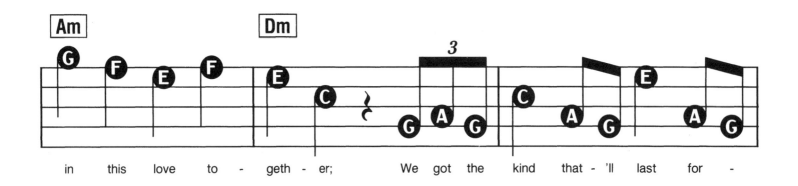

in this love to - geth - er; We got the kind that - 'll last for -

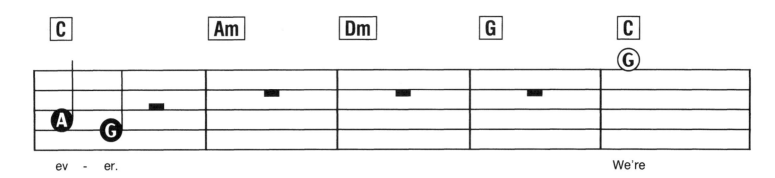

ev - er. We're

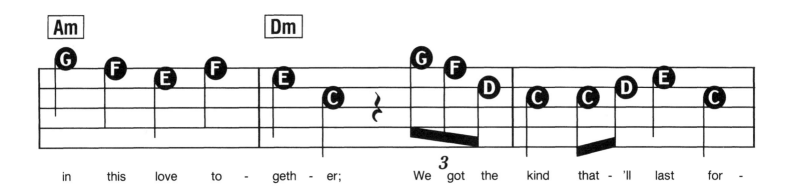

in this love to - geth - er; We got the kind that - 'll last for -

Repeat and Fade

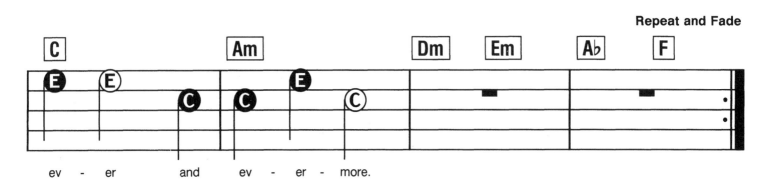

ev - er and ev - er - more.

When a Man Loves a Woman

Registration 4
Rhythm: Waltz or Slow Rock

Words and Music by Calvin Lewis
and Andrew Wright

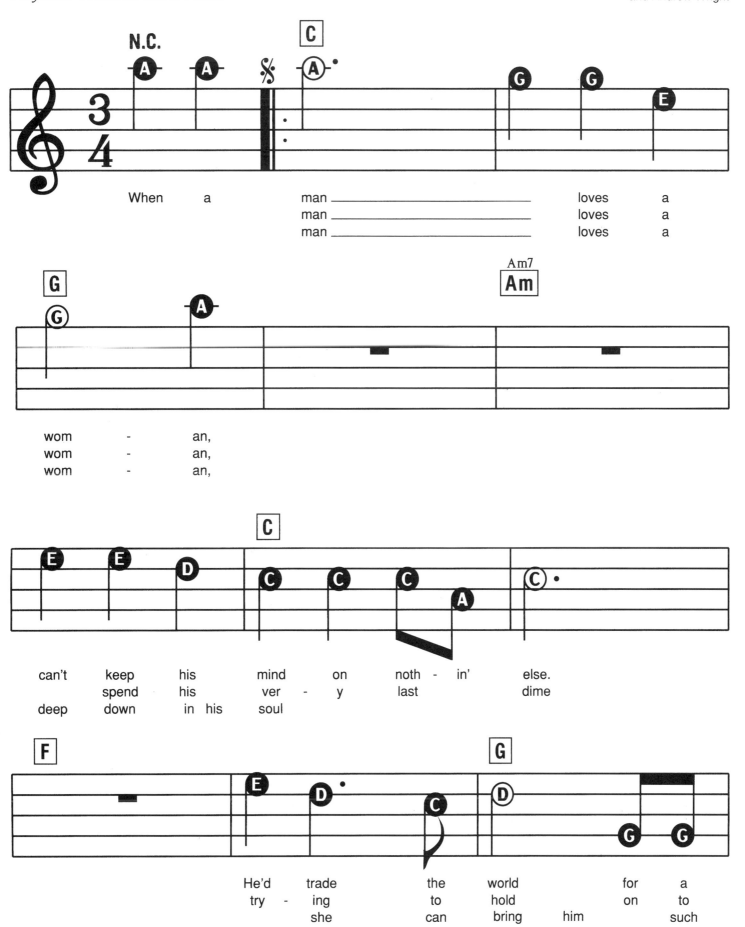

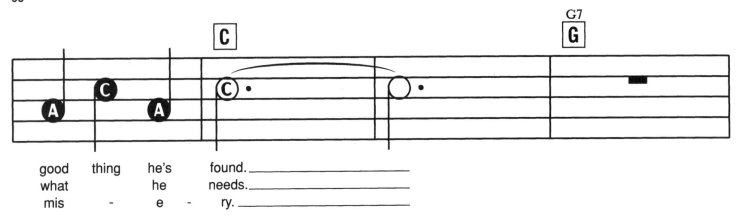

good thing he's found._____
what he needs._____
mis - e - ry._____

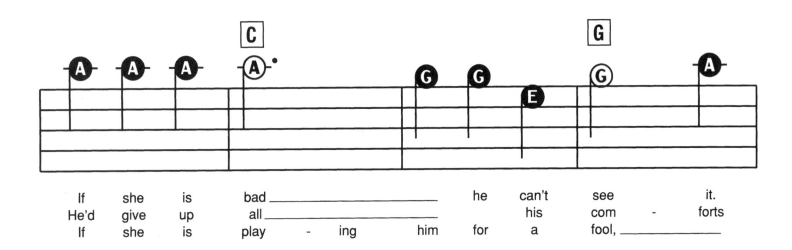

If she is bad_____ he can't see it.
He'd give up all_____ his com - forts
If she is play - ing him for a fool,_____

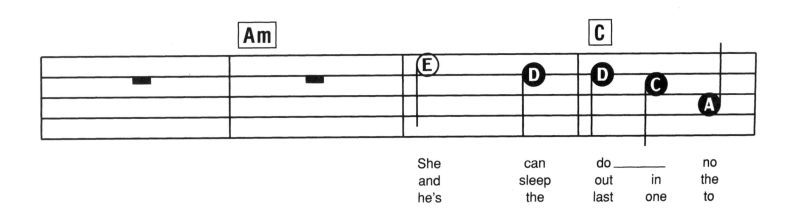

She can do_____ no
and sleep out in the
he's the last one to

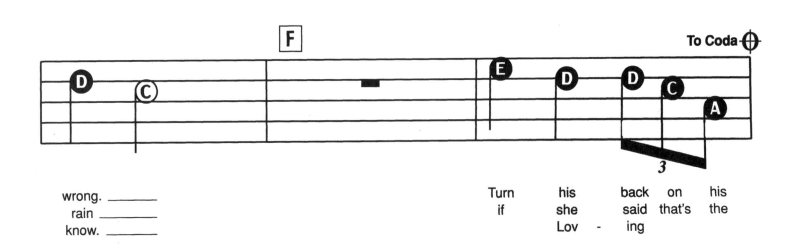

wrong. _____
rain _____
know. _____

Turn his back on his
if she said that's the
Lov - ing

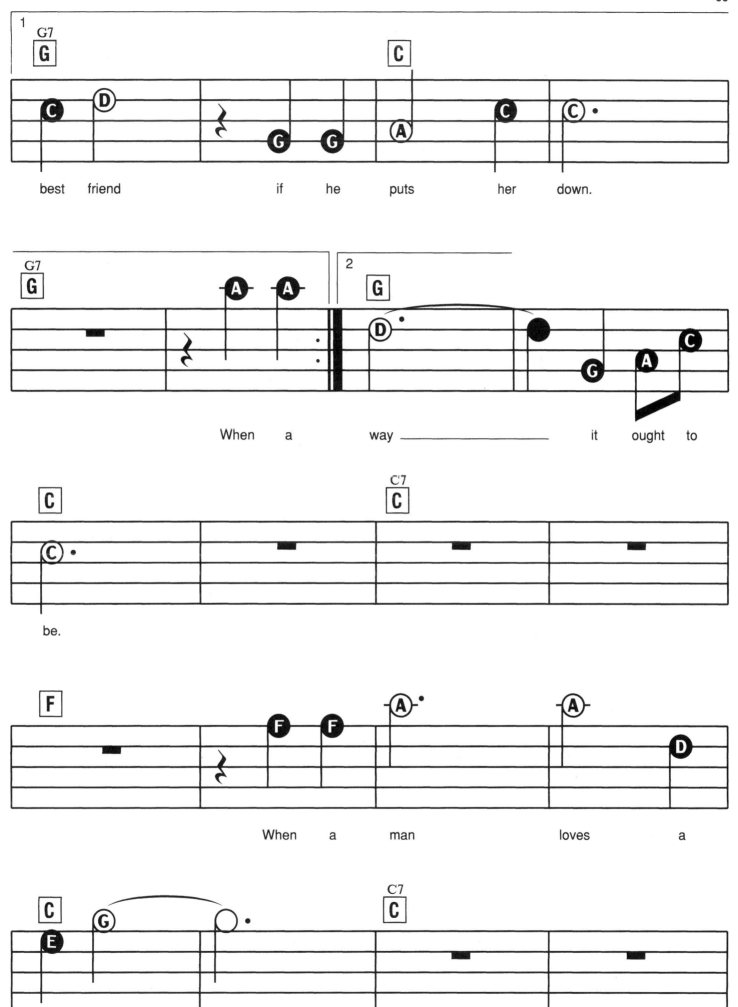

best friend   if he puts her down.

When a way _____ it ought to

be.

When a man loves a

wom - an, _____

100

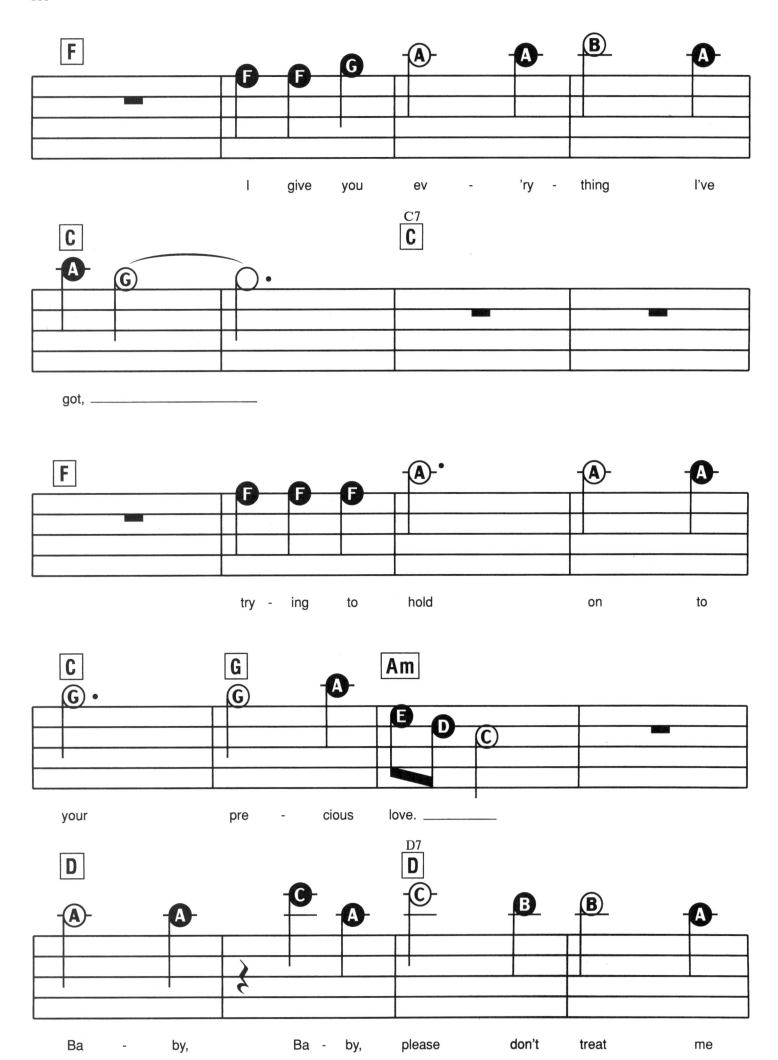

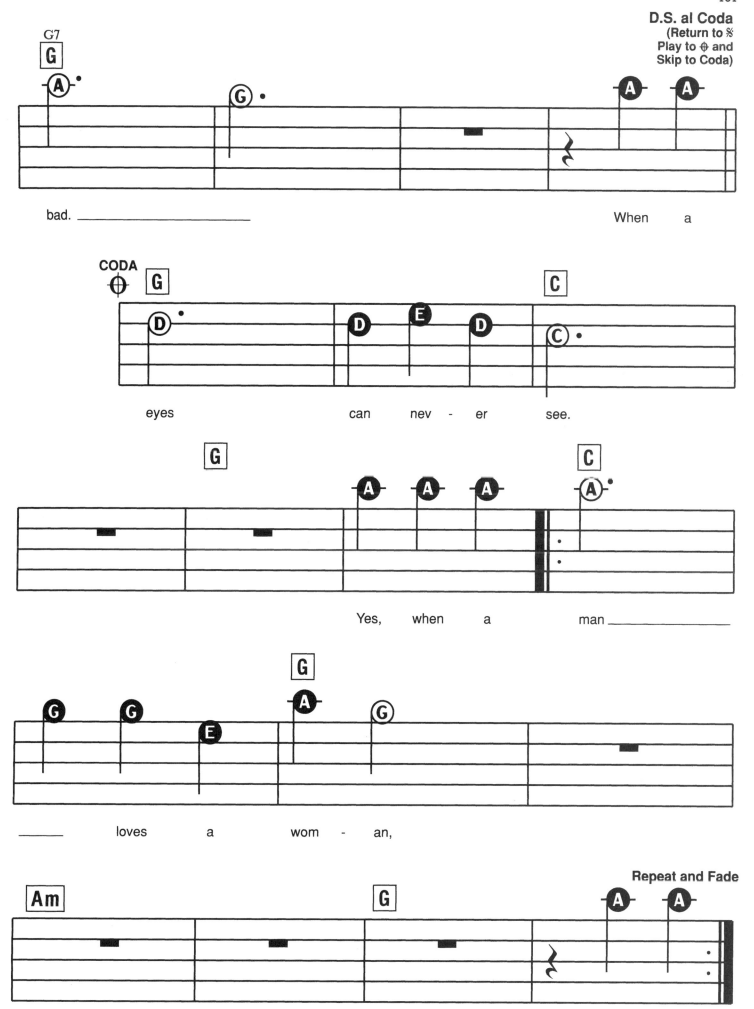

What Are You Doing the Rest of Your Life?

Registration 2
Rhythm: Bossa or Rock

Lyrics by Alan and Marilyn Bergman
Music by Michel Legrand

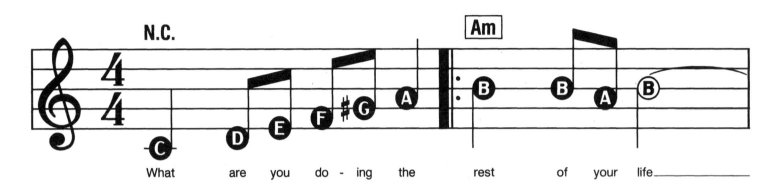

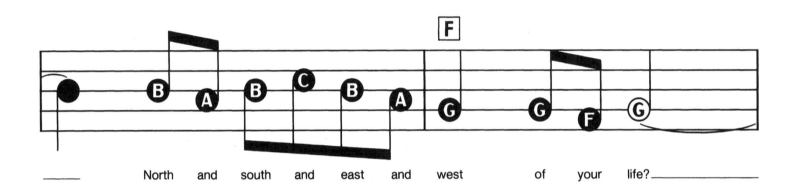

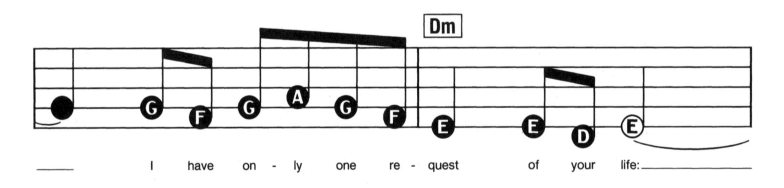

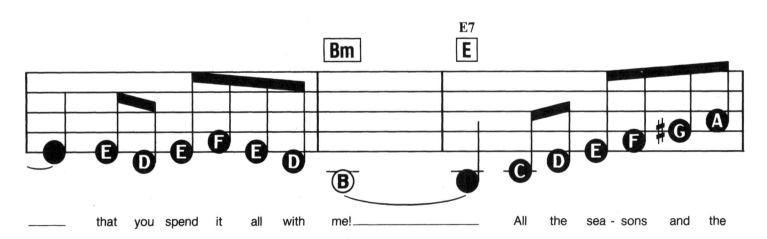

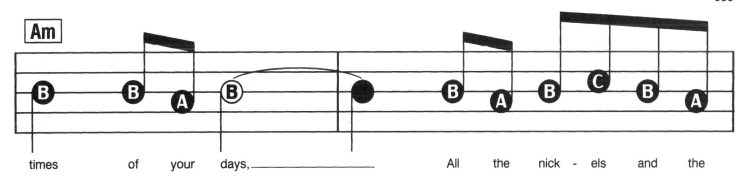

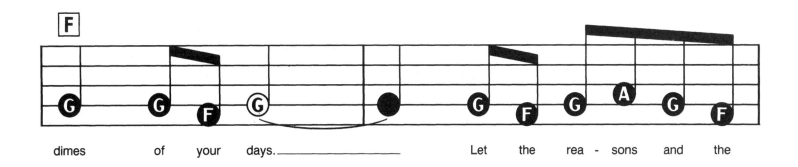

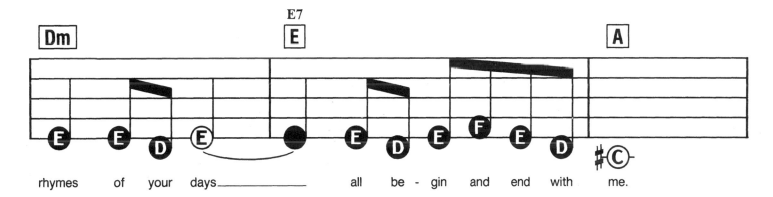

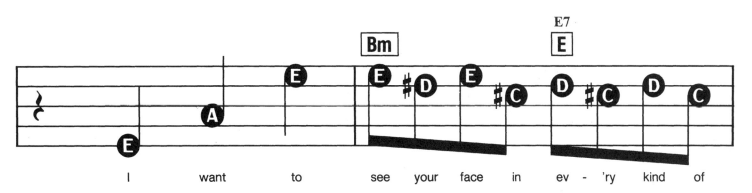

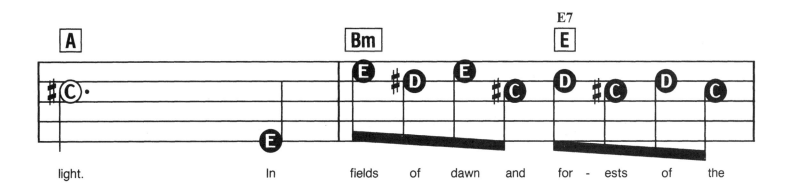

104

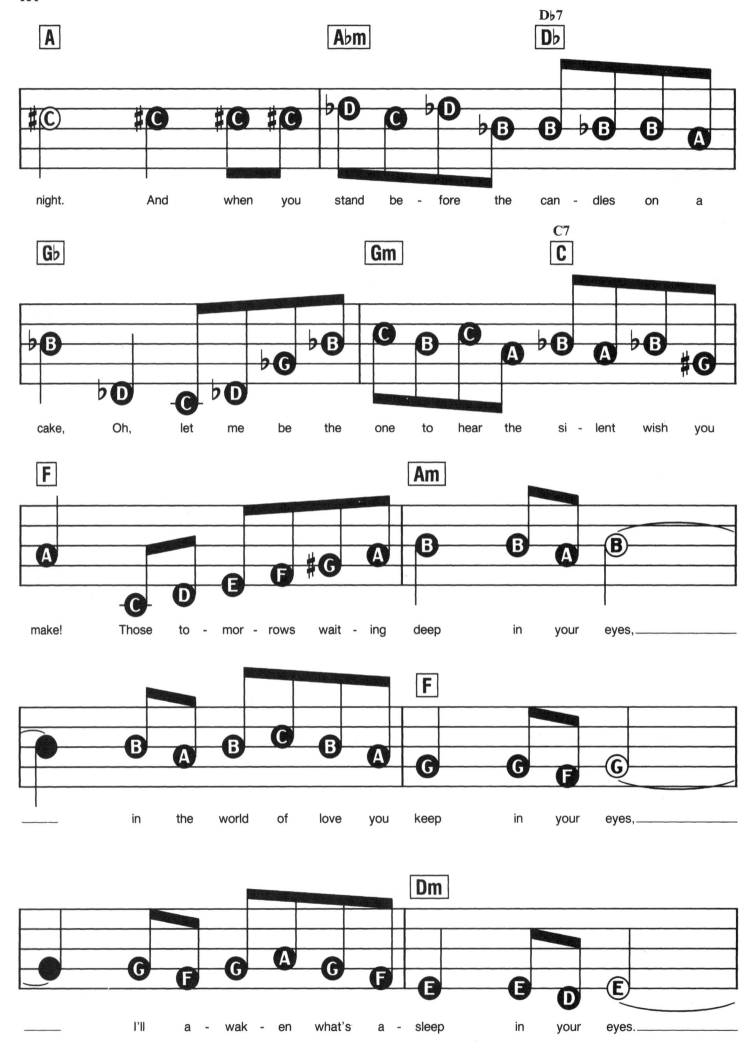

105

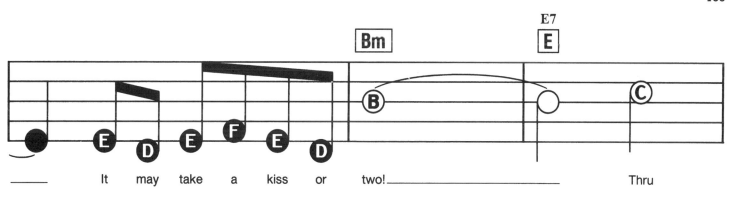

It may take a kiss or two! _____ Thru

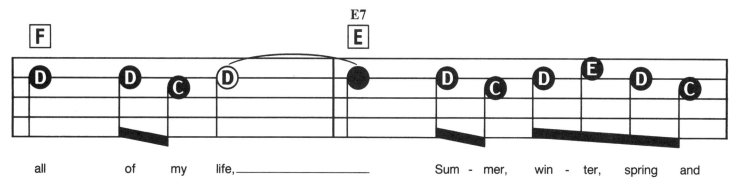

all of my life, _____ Sum - mer, win - ter, spring and

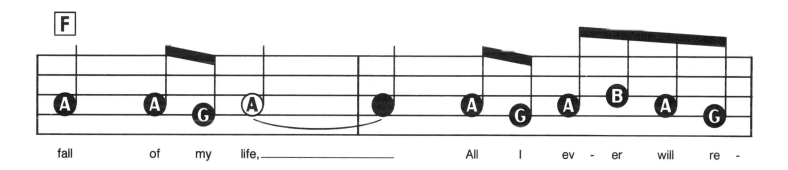

fall of my life, _____ All I ev - er will re -

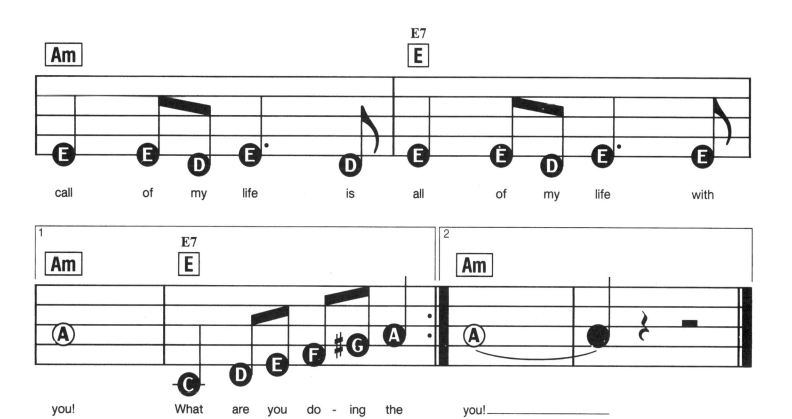

call of my life is all of my life with

you! What are you do - ing the you! _____

You Stepped Out of a Dream

from the M-G-M Picture ZIEGFELD GIRL

Registration 7
Rhythm: Bossa Nova or Pops

Words by Gus Kahn
Music by Nacio Herb Brown

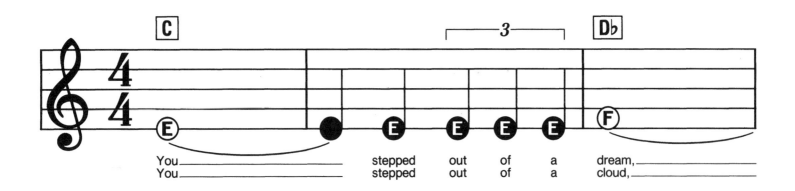

You_____ stepped out of a dream,_____
You_____ stepped out of a cloud,_____

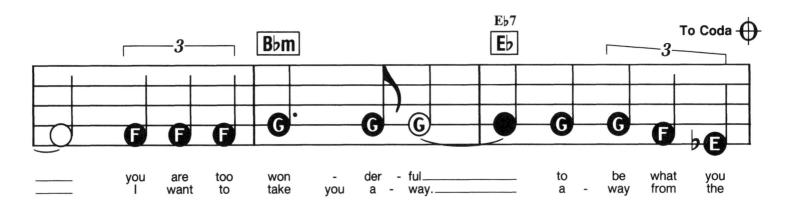

_____ you are too won - der - ful_____ to be what you
_____ I want to take you a - way._____ a - way from the

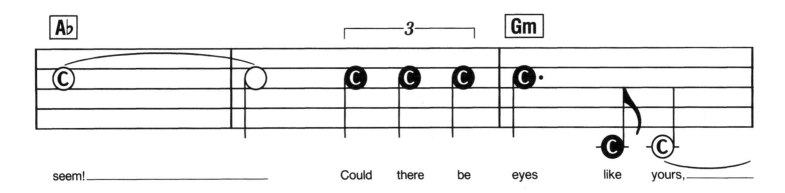

seem!_____ Could there be eyes like yours,_____

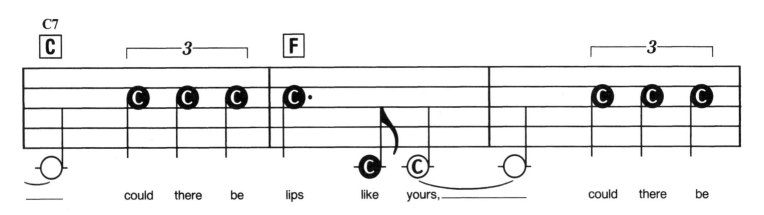

could there be lips like yours,_____ could there be

D.C. al Coda
(Return to beginning
Play to ⊕ and
skip to Coda)

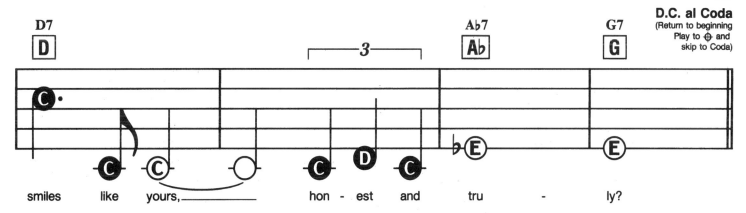

smiles like yours,_____ hon - est and tru - ly?

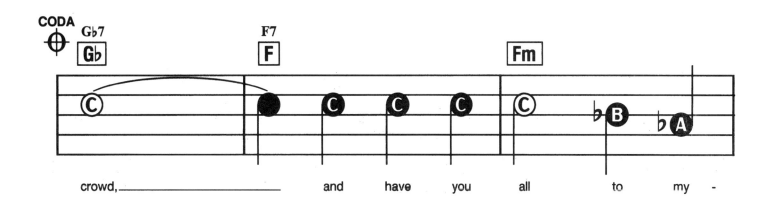

crowd,_____ and have you all to my -

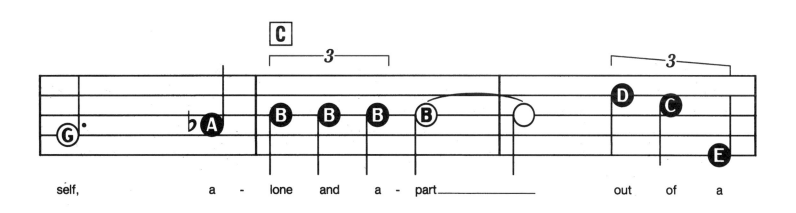

self, a - lone and a - part_____ out of a

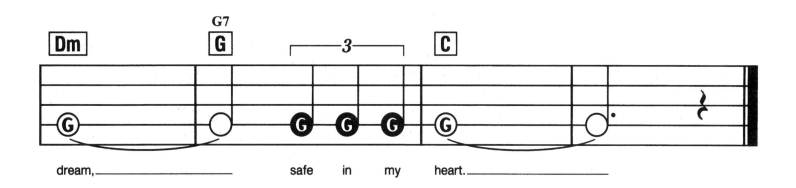

dream,_____ safe in my heart._____

You're Getting to Be a Habit With Me

Registration 8
Rhythm: Jazz or Swing

Lyrics by Al Dubin
Music by Harry Warren

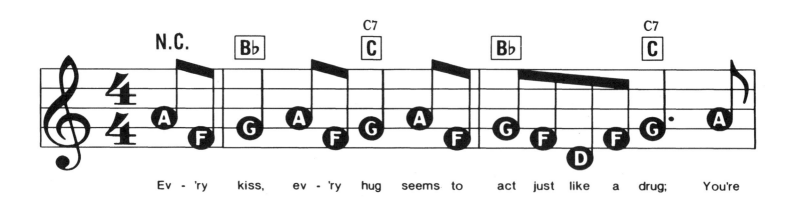

Ev - 'ry kiss, ev - 'ry hug seems to act just like a drug; You're

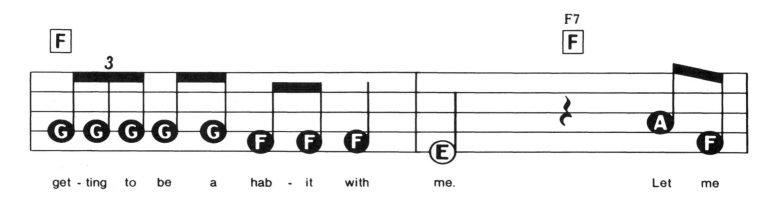

get - ting to be a hab - it with me. Let me

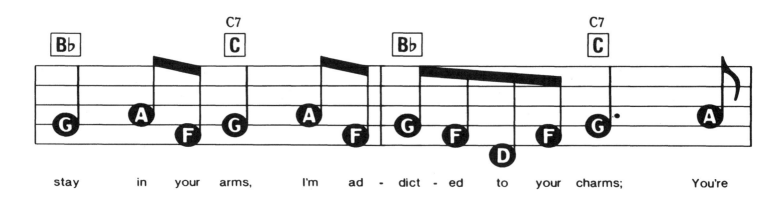

stay in your arms, I'm ad - dict - ed to your charms; You're

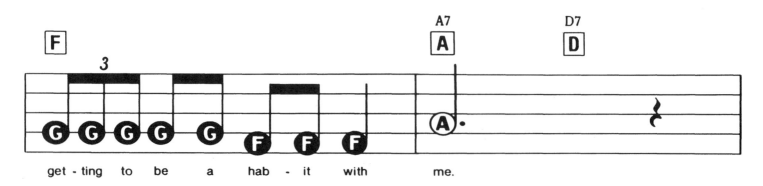

get - ting to be a hab - it with me.

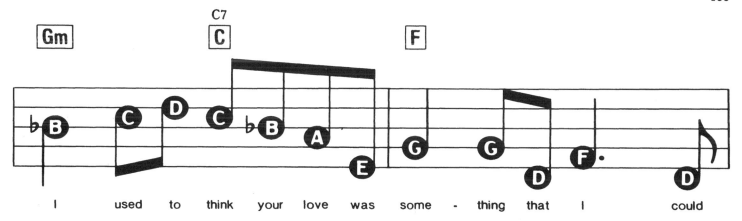

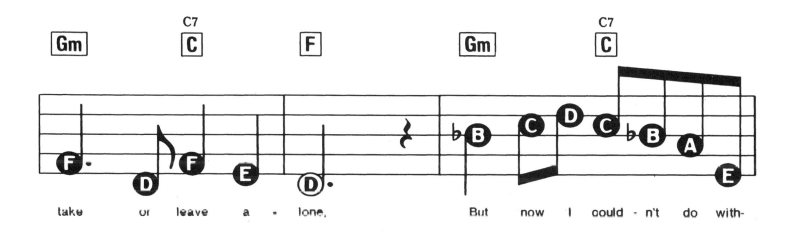

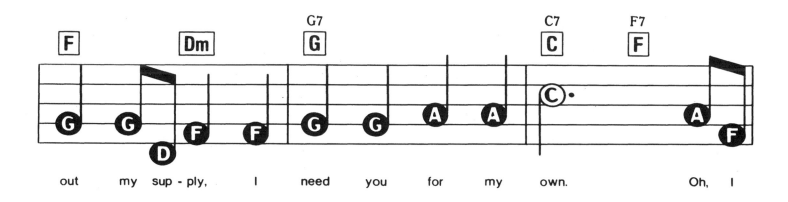

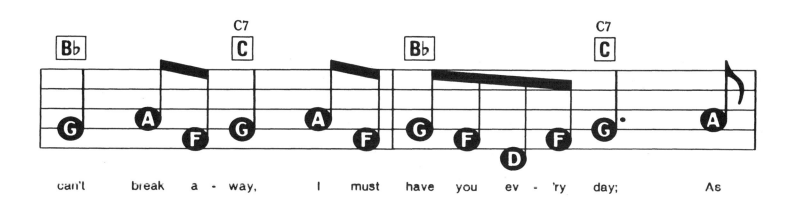

110

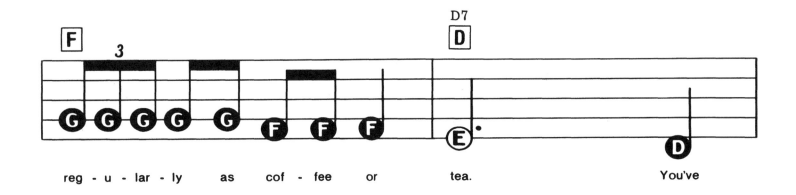

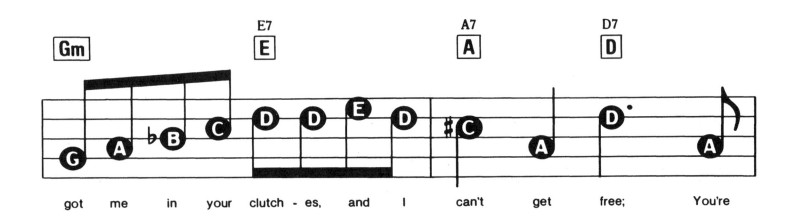

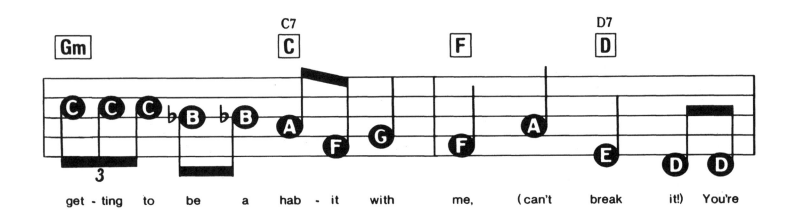

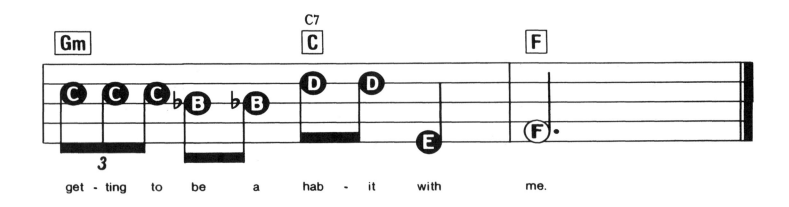

Registration Guide

- Match the Registration number on the song to the corresponding numbered category below. Select and activate an instrumental sound available on your instrument.

- Choose an automatic rhythm appropriate to the mood and style of the song. (Consult your Owner's Guide for proper operation of automatic rhythm features.)

- Adjust the tempo and volume controls to comfortable settings.

Registration

1	Mellow	Flutes, Clarinet, Oboe, Flugel Horn, Trombone, French Horn, Organ Flutes
2	Ensemble	Brass Section, Sax Section, Wind Ensemble, Full Organ, Theater Organ
3	Strings	Violin, Viola, Cello, Fiddle, String Ensemble, Pizzicato, Organ Strings
4	Guitars	Acoustic/Electric Guitars, Banjo, Mandolin, Dulcimer, Ukulele, Hawaiian Guitar
5	Mallets	Vibraphone, Marimba, Xylophone, Steel Drums, Bells, Celesta, Chimes
6	Liturgical	Pipe Organ, Hand Bells, Vocal Ensemble, Choir, Organ Flutes
7	Bright	Saxophones, Trumpet, Mute Trumpet, Synth Leads, Jazz/Gospel Organs
8	Piano	Piano, Electric Piano, Honky Tonk Piano, Harpsichord, Clavi
9	Novelty	Melodic Percussion, Wah Trumpet, Synth, Whistle, Kazoo, Perc. Organ
10	Bellows	Accordion, French Accordion, Mussette, Harmonica, Pump Organ, Bagpipes

FOR ORGANS, PIANOS & ELECTRONIC KEYBOARDS

E-Z PLAY® TODAY PUBLICATIONS

The E-Z Play® Today songbook series is the shortest distance between beginning music and playing fun! Check out this list of highlights and visit www.halleonard.com for a complete listing of all volumes and songlists.

HAL•LEONARD® CORPORATION

7777 W. BLUEMOUND RD. P.O. BOX 13819 MILWAUKEE, WI 53213

Prices, contents, and availability subject to change without notice.

0315